Northwest Historical Series
XII

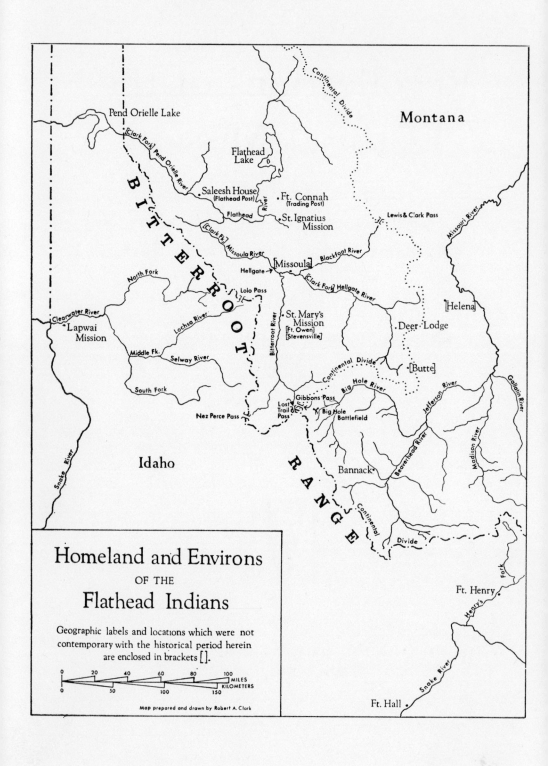

Pend Orielle Lake

[Clark Fork] Pend Orielle River

Flathead
Lake

Continental Divide

Montana

Missouri River

BITTERROOT

Saleesh House
(Flathead Post)

Ft. Connah
(Trading Post)

Flathead

River

St. Ignatius
Mission

Lewis & Clark Pass

[Clark Fk]

Missoula River

Missoula

Hellgate→

Blackfoot River

North Fork

Lolo Pass

[Clark Fork] Hellgate River

Helena

Clearwater River

Lochsa River

St. Mary's
Mission
[Ft. Owen]
[Stevensville]

Deer Lodge

Lapwai
Mission

Bitterroot River

Middle Fk.

Selway River

Continental Divide

[Butte]

South Fork

RANGE

Big Hole River

Jefferson River

Gallatin River

Nez Perce Pass

Lost
Trail
Pass

Gibbons Pass

Big Hole
Battlefield

Idaho

Bannack

Beaverhead River

Madison River

Snake River

Continental

Divide

Ft. Henry

Henry's Fork

Homeland and Environs

OF THE

Flathead Indians

Geographic labels and locations which were not
contemporary with the historical period herein
are enclosed in brackets [].

0   20   40   60   80   100
                                          MILES
                                          KILOMETERS
0   50   100   150

Map prepared and drawn by Robert A. Clark

Snake River

Ft. Hall

Recollections of the Flathead Mission

Containing Brief Observations
both Ancient and Contemporary
Concerning this Particular Nation

by

FR. GREGORY MENGARINI, S.J.

Translated and Edited with
a Biographical Introduction
by
GLORIA RICCI LOTHROP

THE ARTHUR H. CLARK COMPANY
Glendale, California
1977

AD MATREM ET MAGISTRUM

Contents

Illustrations

Preface

Relentless scholarly research best describes the process by which the "Memorie" of Gregory Mengarini,
S.J., was discovered and eventually made available.[1]
The observations of this pioneering Jesuit missionary
to the Flathead Indians, written during his sojourn
with them in the Bitterroot Valley during the 1840s
constitute a significant contribution to frontier ethnology. The translation of this singularly important
document in the history of the Transmontane West
would never have occurred had it not been for the
painstaking investigation of sources by Professor Doyce
B. Nunis, Jr., of the University of Southern California
and the late William L. Davis, S.J., of Gonzaga University. In 1960 the existence of this manuscript was
unknown to Western history scholars. But questions
raised by Professor Nunis, as he edited the memoirs
of Josiah Belden, necessarily included queries about
the Jesuit missionaries, including Mengarini, with
whom Belden's group traveled for many weeks in the

---

[1] Gregory Mengarini, "Memorie delle Missioni delle Teste Piatte contenenti
brevi nozioni cosi antiche che moderne di tutto cio che riguarda questa na-
zione in particulare," Montes Saxosi, Vol. 1, Fol. VIII, p. 7 ff, General Archives
of the Society of Jesus, Rome, Italy. (Hereinafter cited as Mt. Sax., GASJ.)

first planned 1841 emigrant party to strike overland for
California. The questions raised spurred inquiry, for
they needed answers.

Naturally, the investigation was enthusiastically
aided by Father Davis, an authority on the history of
the Society of Jesus in the Northwest, and a specialist
particularly on the life of Pierre Jean De Smet, S.J.
Eventually, the combined research bore fruit. On January 22, 1961, Father Davis wrote: "I have not yet told
you of the great discovery I have made. . . Among
the [Gilbert J.] Garraghan transcripts at Loyola U.
(Chicago) I found a long narrative account of St.
Mary's mission by Padre Mengarini, S.J." [2]

Father Davis sent a copy of this typescript to Professor Nunis who had provided the initial historical
statements on Mengarini in his introduction to the
edited memoirs of Josiah Belden.[3] As a result of the
generosity of both Father Davis and Professor Nunis,
the "Memorie" was made available to me as the basis
for my doctoral dissertation. I snapped the lure; this
finished endeavor, I hope, warrants the confidence and
enthusiastic support placed in me by the late Father
Davis and Professor Nunis.

Through the additional assistance of these two leading Western historians, it was also possible to continue
research in the Jesuit Provincial Archives at Gonzaga
University. There a microfilm copy was discovered of
the original manuscript which is housed in Rome.
After a careful comparison of the original handwritten

2 William L. Davis, S.J., to Doyce B. Nunis, Jr., Evanston, Ill., Jan. 22,
1961, personal corr. file, courtesy of Doyce B. Nunis, Jr.

3 Doyce B. Nunis, Jr. (ed.), *Josiah Belden, 1841 California Overland Pioneer*, p. 25. (All pertinent works are listed in full in bibliography.)

text and the typescript, numerous errors in the latter
were corrected. The document was then translated and
edited.

It is true that there are obvious parallels between the
"Memorie" and Mengarini's later reminiscences such
as "The Rocky Mountains," originally published in
The Woodstock Letters, and subsequently edited by
Albert J. Partoll as "Mengarini's Narrative of the
Rockies." [4] It has also been noted that before his death,
the aging Jesuit dictated his memoirs, which were then
published in a limited edition for private circulation.[5]
In the *Woodstock* edition of the memoirs, however,
Mengarini introduces the narrative with the observation: "Now when I am old and life's shortening steps
hurry me toward the tomb, I am asked to stop awhile
and tell the story of the birth, infancy, and premature
death of the earliest of the Rocky Mountain missions." [6]

In contrast, the original reminiscences were written
while the thirty-seven-year-old missionary was serving
at St. Mary's mission. Thus the impressions are firsthand, precise and vivid. The accuracy of the date and
hence the validity of the data are assured by the fact that
in the final paragraphs of the account Mengarini outlined his future plans for the expansion of the settlement, describing in detail the trees, meadows and crude

---

4 Gregory Mengarini, "The Rocky Mountains, The Memoirs of Father
Gregory Mengarini," *The Woodstock Letters,* xvii (1888), pp. 293-309; xviii
(1889), pp. 25-43, 142-53; ed. by Albert J. Partoll, "Mengarini's Narrative of
the Rockies," *Frontier and Midland,* xviii (Spring 1938), pp. 193-202; (Summer 1938), 258-266.

5 "In 1884 while serving on the faculty of Santa Clara College, Father
Mengarini acceded to the requests of several Jesuit friends and dictated this
account. A few copies were printed after his death on September 23, 1886."
Nunis, *Belden,* p. 25.

6 Mengarini, "The Rocky Mountains," *The Woodstock Letters,* xvii, p. 298.

brick houses. He added that the mission's progress and expansion were outlined on an attached map which long since has been lost.

The "Memorie" acquired even greater significance when compared to similar journals and diaries of the period. Unlike the brilliantly illustrated *Wilderness Kingdom,* the memoirs of Mengarini's Jesuit companion, Nicolas Point,[7] the following account is concerned with a variety of ethnographic elements and anthropological factors, as well as with spiritual victories and disappointments. Mengarini's narrative thus assumes an ethnohistorical dimension.

Furthermore, since Father Mengarini spent nearly an entire decade with the Flatheads, his text offers a long range view of the diminution of cultic practices, the modification of familial relationships, and the marked changes in governmental and economic patterns. One might venture that on this basis Mengarini was justified in expressing an hypothesis regarding the acculturative influences of the advancing whites upon the native Indian. One might add further that where the accounts penned by De Smet provide the grand panorama, Mengarini's provide the case study.

There is an added significance in this work. Few men know of Gregory Mengarini. Fewer still would include his name on the list of westward trailblazers. Yet this patrician young Roman, aquiline in profile and firm of jaw, was among the vanguard of westering pioneers. His missionary group was accompanied for many weeks by the first wagon train to California led by John Bidwell. After the two companies separated at Soda

---

[7] Nicolas Point, *Wilderness Kingdom, Indian Life in the Rocky Mountains,* trans. and ed. by Joseph P. Donnelly, s.j.

Springs on the Bear River, it was Gregory Mengarini who became the administrative head of the first Jesuit mission in the Rockies. He directed the planting of the first seeds, and participated in the erection of the first log church, built in a protected valley, twenty-eight miles from the mouth of the Bitterroot River. His long, bitterly cold nights were spent compiling the first Salish or Flathead grammar, as well as transcribing the beginnings of a Salishan dictionary.[8]

With the closing of St. Mary's mission in 1850, Mengarini was to participate in launching yet another "first." He soon joined Fathers Nobili and Accolti to assist in the organization of the first permanent college in California at Santa Clara. During more than half a century this Jesuit labored in the United States never far removed from the thin advance line of the frontier settlement. Part of his task was to nourish the culture and the traditions that struggled to survive along the wilderness trail. His commitment to his Faith and his devoted service to white and Indian alike were to draw him across the continent from Baltimore, to Westport, and finally to the Pacific coast of California.

In translating and editing this western pioneer's narrative, certain liberties were necessarily taken. Idio-

---

[8] According to Carlos Sommervogel, ed., *Bibliotheque de la Compagnie de Jesus,* v, p. 946, Mengarini's publications include the following: *A Salishan or Flathead Grammar* (New York, 1861); "Vocabulary of the Shwoyelpi, Schitzui and Salish Proper," *Contributions to American Ethnology,* ed. by John Wesley Powell (Wash., 1877), I, pp. 248-65, 267-85; "Indians of Oregon," *Journal of Anthropological Research of New York* (New York, 1871-72), I, pp. 81-88; "Letter to P. De Smet, Saint Mary's, June 28, 1842," in Jean Pierre De Smet, *Voyages aux Montagnes Rocheuses* (New ed., Brussels, 1873), pp. 224-26; "Vocabulary of the Santa Clara Indians," *Cont. to Am. Ethn.,* ed. by John Wesley Powell (Wash., 1877), III, pp. 538-49; "The Rocky Mountains, The Memoirs of Father Gregory Mengarini," *The Woodstock Letters,* XVII & XVIII.

matic expressions were modernized. While the author's style was respected in an attempt to retain the "flavor" of the account, transposition of phrase and a change in sentence structure were occasionally required for the sake of clarity. In the interests of organization, paragraphing and the division of the account into chapters were allowed.

For the opportunity to translate and edit the "Memorie," I am indebted to the late Father Davis and to Professor Nunis who encouraged me to first undertake this research as the basis of my doctoral dissertation, made possible by a Haynes Dissertation Fellowship awarded by the University of Southern California, 1967-68. For access to the entire catalogue of Father Mengarini's correspondence in the Jesuit Archives in Rome, I am indebted to Father Joseph Fejer, S.J., of the *Archivum Romanum Societatis Jesu*. For many other related items, I thank Father Wilfred A. Schoenberg, S.J., Director of the Jesuit Provincial Archives, Crosby Library, Gonzaga University.

For the greater part of the biographical data I wish to acknowledge my debt to the Jesuit Provincial Archives, Spokane, Washington; the California State Library; the Jesuit Archives of the California Province, Palo Alto; and the *Archivum Romanum Societatis Jesu* in Rome.

Thanks are extended to Miss Mary Isabel Fry of the Henry E. Huntington Library; Mrs. Charlotte Tufts, formerly the librarian of the Southwest Museum; Mrs. Elizabeth Crahan of the Los Angeles County Medical Association Library; and Miss Josephine L. Harper of the State Historical Society of Wisconsin, Madison.

Not to be forgotten is Harold D. Roberson, Superintendent of the Flathead Indian Agency, Jocko Indian Reservation, who introduced me to the Bitterroot Valley and arranged for my attendance at a Flathead tribal council meeting. And to Samuel K. Lothrop, a sigh of relief and appreciative thanks for his unfaltering aeronautic skills which transported us to the various mission sites across land as desolate and ranges as rugged as Mengarini described.

Also, sincere thanks to Gerald Ingham of Loyola University, and to my mother, Mrs. Maria Angeli Ricci, who immeasurably eased the burden of translation from four languages.

To all, my heartfelt thanks.

GLORIA RICCI LOTHROP
Pasadena, California

Part I
Introduction

THE SOCIETY OF JESUS

Pioneering Priests on a Moving Frontier

By the end of the fifteenth century Europe's westward pursuit of empire was coupled with missionary advances across the northern and southern reaches of the newly discovered land. Among the most zealous were the followers of Ignatius of Loyola. Shortly after his organization of the Society of Jesus, the Jesuits were preaching and converting under the flags of competing imperial powers in the New World.

With the sanction of the Viceroy of New Spain, the Society extended its efforts from the Gulf of Mexico to Baja California, and in 1595 established the College and Seminary of San José in Manila. To the north Jesuits arrived in Port Royal, Acadia in 1611. During the next four decades the Society organized missions along the Atlantic coast, on the banks of the St. Lawrence, on the shores of Hudson's Bay, and as far south as the Gulf of Mexico. For a few brief years until the Glorious Revolution of 1688, the Jesuits were allowed to publicly conduct their ministries in the British colonies of Maryland and Pennsylvania.

On July 21, 1773, however, Pope Clement XIV acceded to political pressure and issued the Brief of

Suppression against the Society of Jesus. The suppression extended across the known world leaving only a few Jesuits at isolated outposts under the protective rule of Catherine the Great of Russia, and Prussia's Emporer Frederick who confided to Voltaire that he would safeguard the Jesuits, and thus maintain "the precious seed so that someday I may supply it to those who may cultivate that rare plant in their countries." [1]

Finally, in August 1814, Pope Pius VII restored the Society of Jesus. Moved by the recommendations of Tsar Paul I, King Ferdinand of the Kingdom of the Two Sicilies, and the almost unanimous request of the Christian world now fully recognizant of the richly fruitful successes of the Jesuits, they were again permitted "to serve the Pope throughout the whole world at whatsoever task he should wish to assign." [2]

Following the restoration of the Society, its missionary activities advanced to the uncharted reaches of the globe, as far indeed as the forested wilderness of the Oregon Country. During these same years the political climate in Europe had forced Jesuits to turn ever more toward the mission fields.[3] Belgian Jesuits, for example, were unable to return to their homeland until its separation from Holland in 1830. During the upheavals in France in 1830 which toppled Charles X, mobs sacked several French novitiates. Only a few years before, Jesuits had been murdered and others beaten in the mistaken belief that they had caused an epidemic of

[1] Thomas J. Campbell, s.j., *The Jesuits, 1534-1921,* II, p. 637.

[2] Michael P. Harney, s.j., *The Jesuits in History,* pp. 330-39.

[3] As a result of the small proportion of religious vocations to the total Catholic population, the United States was considered a missionary field until the middle of the twentieth century.

cholera which ravaged parts of Spain.[4] Upheavals in
several emerging nation states, particularly Italy, accounted for the international roster of the Society in
the United States.

Although political unrest in Europe served to staff
missions abroad, the years immediately following the
restoration of the Society were bleak with no apparent
surcease. Resources were so limited that the Fathers
were hard put to maintain long-established parishes in
Maryland and Pennsylvania. The fate of their college
at Georgetown was even more problematic. For lack of
funds, a band of Belgian youths who had entered the
novitiate at Whitemarsh nearly faced dismissal. Not
until the 1840s with its avalanche of immigrants from
the Catholic countries of Western Europe could the
Jesuits dare anticipate expansion in the growing urban
centers, albeit while enduring the menaces of nascent
"know-nothingism."

At the same time fortuitous developments in the mission fields of the middle United States provided new
challenges for the Jesuit apostolate. Bishop Louis
William du Bourg, administrator of New Orleans,
while in Rome for his episcopal consecration in 1815,
first requested Jesuit priests for his far-flung diocese of
Louisiana. The frontier bishopric consisted of the territory west of the Mississippi, reaching indefinitely to the
northwest and comprising the bulk of the Indian territory. The diocese itself was bounded by the dioceses of
Kentucky and Florida on the east and the "Sea of the
South" to the west.

It was not until 1833 that the pleas of yet another

[4] Campbell, *The Jesuits,* II, pp. 738-64.

bishop of New Orleans, Antoine Blanc, persuaded
Father General John Roothaan to assign four young
Jesuits to the vast diocese. Among these were Father
Nicolas Point, then in Spain, and Father Anthony
Eysvogels. The latter was to be assigned to the Pot-
awatomi mission of St. Joseph. Father Point was des-
tined to join Fathers Pierre Jean De Smet and Gregory
Mengarini among the Flatheads.[5]

A decade earlier a handful of Jesuits had already
returned to work among the Indians after a fifty-year
absence. At the urging of Secretary of War John C.
Calhoun, Bishop du Bourg proposed to Father Charles
Van Quickenborne,[6] Master of Novices at Whitemarsh,
that he would be given a tract of land near the episcopal
see at St. Louis if the Jesuits would establish a novitiate
there.[7]

The company headed by Van Quickenborne set out
from Whitemarsh in April 1823. Three wagons carried
personal articles as far as Wheeling on the Ohio River,
where the group purchased two flatboats. The company
of twelve, however, made the entire trip *"pedibus*

---

[5] Requests for Jesuits were usually met with the response that the members
of the Society were either too young or too old for such work, since the training of priests had been brought to a virtual standstill during the Suppression.
Thomas Hughes, *History of the Society of Jesus in North America, Colonial
and Federal Documents,* I, pp. 107-10.

[6] Rev. Charles Felix Van Quickenborne was the first Jesuit to enter the
Mississippi Valley after the re-establishment of the Society. Hiram M. Chit-
tenden and Alfred D. Richardson, eds., *Life, Letters and Travels of Father
Pierre Jean De Smet,* 1801-1872, I, p. 151.

[7] Calhoun's actions can be explained in part by the fact that issues relating
to Indian affairs fell under the jurisdiction of the War Department, although
not as a separate bureau until 1824. Furthermore, it was assumed that the
removal of the Indians would appear less inhumane, and they in turn, more
quiescent if ministered to by a Christian missionary. William T. Hagan,
American Indians, pp. 74-79.

apostolorum, staff in hand", as Father De Smet expressed it.[8] The seven novices, three lay brothers and two priests finally arrived at what was to be their new novitiate at Florissant. There they found more pressing work among the whites, now pouring into the new country and forming settlements in Missouri and Illinois. At one settlement Van Quickenborne discovered six hundred Catholics where only eight had been reported. Almost immediately, the Society established St. Louis College and soon after St. Xavier's College in Cincinnati.

Among the tasks accomplished by the small group was a project which had been outlined by De Smet. Though still five years from ordination, he wanted work – missionary work – to be achieved by building a boarding school for Indian boys where not only catechism, but reading, writing, spelling, tool forging, blacksmithing and carpentry would be taught. The plan appeared feasible to General William Clark, Superintendent of Indian Affairs for the federal government in the area. He stirred the interest of Andrew Jackson in the White House, and soon Secretary of War Calhoun signed an appropriation for the support of St. Regis Seminary.[9]

As funds diminished, however, and the Indians loaded their ponies and pulled their teepees farther west, De Smet heard the empty echo of defeat. He was to hear it again at the mission to the Kickapoo, and later among the Potawatomies, before crossing the Divide and claiming his place in history.

Upon De Smet's return in 1837 from a four-year

---

[8] Chittenden and Richardson, *De Smet,* I, p. 5.
[9] Harney, *Jesuits in History,* pp. 403-04.

assignment in Europe, the young priest was chosen to serve as resident missionary to two thousand Potawatomi Indians recently settled along the Missouri River in what was later the Nebraska Territory. Senator Thomas Hart Benton of Missouri and General Clark, with the support of President Martin Van Buren, were in favor of a proposal to send a Jesuit to reside with the tribesmen, hoping he would provide a sufficiently powerful scourge against the "blood-wild" neighboring Sioux, the gambling, laziness and the whiskey. "When the Potawatomies received their government pension money, they poured it out for liquor; and after the cash was gone, they bartered blankets, horses, food – even their own children – for drink." Those who visited the uprooted natives of the land noted that when they secured the white man's drink, "they murdered and mutilated – hacking at each other's ears and noses with bloody knives." [10]

In addition to the distress the Jesuit missionary felt at being surrounded by examples of superstition, polygamy and plague, he expressed particular distress at the neglected condition of the children, adding: "Their hair seems never to have undergone the operations of a brush so that their heads look like masses of cobwebs. Many have eye trouble, and their faces and all their limbs look as if water never touched them." [11]

It was during the second year at St. Mary's mission

---

[10] Michael McHugh, s.j., "A Dream Went West," *I Lift My Lamp, Jesuits in America*, ed. by John P. Leary, s.j., p. 162. Andrew M. Jung, *Jesuit Missions Among the American Tribes of the Rocky Mountain Indians*, deals extensively with the subject.

[11] Chittenden and Richardson, *De Smet*, I, p. 158; William L. Davis, s.j., "Peter John De Smet: Missionary to the Potawatomi, 1837-1840," *Pacific Northwest Quar.*, XXXII (Apr. 1942), pp. 123-52.

among the Potawatomi, near Council Bluffs, that two
strange Indians disembarked upon the muddy bank of
the Missouri. In recounting that first meeting with
Pierre Gaucher and Young Ignace, De Smet recalled,
"I have never seen any savages so fervent in religion."
The two visitors explained that during the twenty-three
years they had dwelt with the Flatheads and the Nez
Perce, the tribesmen had learned "to strictly observe
Sunday and assembled several times a week to pray and
sing the canticles." De Smet gave them letters of recommendation for the Reverend Father Superior in St.
Louis as they departed, "adding another three hundred
leagues to the thousand they had already accomplished." [12]

De Smet's admiration was to mature and provide the
vision for the Mission to the Rocky Mountains. The
two pilgrims had opened to De Smet a horizon of
opportunity for him and for the daring dusty few who
would forge the heartland of the continent to reach the
supplicant Flatheads.

---

[12] Chittenden and Richardson, *De Smet,* I, pp. 29-30.

The Plea From the West

Although the meeting at Council Bluffs was Pierre De Smet's introduction to the zealous Flatheads, this had not been the first plea for priests from the Oregon Country. As early as 1821 Hudson's Bay Company employees, mostly French and Iroquois, dispatched a petition for spiritual aid to Father Joseph Rosati, Vicar-General of Upper Louisiana. His official response was that it was impossible to meet their request at that time. In 1834 this same group petitioned the Catholic hierarchy in Canada to arrange with George Simpson, governor of Rupert's Land of the Hudson's Bay Company domain, for the assignment of a Catholic missionary to serve at the Cowlitz River Station in the Oregon British-American territory.[1] Finally, in 1838 the Very Reverend Francis Norbert Blanchet, Vicar-General to the Bishop of Quebec, with his associate Father Modeste Demers, "crossed the Rockie Mountains through the Athabaska Pass, and descended the Columbia River to Fort Vancouver."[2] There the

---

[1] Clarence B. Bagley, *Early Catholic Missions in Old Oregon*, p. 62.

[2] Major Edward Mallet, "Origin of the Flathead Mission of the Rocky Mountains," *Records of the Cath. Hist. Soc.,* II (1889), p. 196; Gilbert J. Garraghan, *The Jesuits of the Middle United States*, II, p. 271.

two established the first Catholic mission in the Oregon country.

The first notions of Christianity the Northwest Indians acquired appear to have been introduced by the Christian Iroquois of the Caughnawaga mission, perhaps members of the 1811 group in the employ of the Hudson's Bay Company agent, Nicholas Pambrizi. Two decades later, American fur traders, Captain Benjamin L. E. Bonneville and Nathaniel Wyeth, found the Indians well-versed in Christian teachings.

At Fort Colville on November 6, 1838, a large number of Colvilles, Pend d'Oreilles, Spokans and Flatheads flocked to see the French priests. Abbé Blanchet assembled them several times during his three-day stay to instruct them in the elements of religion. Some displayed a particular enthusiasm about the Faith, seeking to acquire their own Black Robe. Imagining that they could buy one, they inquired of the Canadians how many horses and beavers it would take to have one of these "chiefs of the French" stay with them, saying, "He would want for nothing."[3]

An even more dramatic appeal for missionaries was laid before Bishop Rosati and the Jesuits during that same decade – an appeal which culminated in the visit to De Smet at his Potawatomi mission. In 1831, a party of four Indians appeared in St. Louis seeking a Black Robe, as they described the Jesuits, to return with them to the lands of the bitter root. Since the number of priests at the Missouri mission fell altogether below actual needs, the distant enterprise was deemed impos-

---

[3] Bagley, *Early Catholic Missions*, p. 62.

sible, and the delegation's request was turned aside by the Church administrators.

Confusion still surrounds the actual date of this fateful visit as well as the number and composition of the delegation. The eastern press carried reports of an Indian delegation in search of the "White Man's Book of Heaven" arriving in St. Louis in October 1831. Some years later, however, Lucien Fontenelle of the American Fur Company told Marcus Whitman that four Indians of the 1831 delegation had traveled with him. If so, they arrived earlier than October 1, 1831.[4]

Despite the contentions advanced by some recorders of the event that the delegation was composed solely of Nez Perce, it, no doubt, was a joint enterprise involving Flatheads as well. Persuasive proof lies in the official documentation still available. The burial register of the Cathedral of St. Louis indicates that one of the Indians, *"Narcissus Keepeellele, ou Pipe Bard du Nez Perce de la tribu de Chopweek Nation apelle tetes Plates age d'environ quarante ans,"* died the following November 7 and was buried in the same cemetery.[5]

The details of the visit were summarized in a letter written some three weeks later by Bishop Rosati. On December 31, 1831, he embellished the already edifying story, describing in detail the virtuous character of the members of the group, of their religious fervor, as well as their evident familiarity with Catholic ritual.[6] In a letter to Jesuit Father General Roothaan, written on October 20, 1839, Bishop Rosati again outlined the

---

4 Clifford M. Drury, *Marcus and Narcissa Whitman*, I, pp. 37-43.
5 Garraghan, *Jesuits of the Middle United States*, II, p. 237, note 6.
6 *Ibid.*, II, p. 237.

efforts of the Indians to secure the ministrations of a
Catholic priest. He wrote:

> Eight or nine years ago [c. 1831] some of the Flathead nation
> came to St. Louis. The object of their journey was to ascertain if
> the religion spoken of with so much praise by the twenty-four
> Iroquois – the two Iroquois neophytes who settled among the
> Flatheads were accompanied by twenty-two other warriors who
> settled in the country between the Rockies and the Pacific Ocean
> – was in reality such as was represented, and above all if the
> nations that have white skin [the name they had given Europeans]
> had adopted and practiced it.[7]

The fact that the Indians clearly indicated their intentions to Bishop Rosati and later to Fathers De Smet
and Mengarini, their repeated declaration of a desire
to embrace the religion of the Iroquois, and the fact
that they went not to Red River Fort of the Hudson's
Bay Company where some had received Protestant
instruction, but rather had sought out their friend Wil-
lam Clark in St. Louis to support their appeal to the
Bishop, provides a clear indication that the Indians
sought Black Robes or Jesuits and their "High Medicine" of which the Iroquois had spoken. In light of
these facts, their search for the "White Man's Book of
Heaven" reported by the New York *Christian Advocate* represents a figurative interpretation which, with
its emphasis upon the Bible, more typically reflects a
Protestant orientation. The fact that the Flatheads subsequently rejected the ministrations of Whitman and
Spalding, arguing that they did not wear "Black
Gowns" and brought wives with them (*cf* "Memorie,"
Chapter v), further substantiates their faithful adher-
ence to the religion of the Catholic Iroquois.

---

[7] *Ibid.,* II, p. 249.

As early as 1816 Ross Cox, an employee of the North West Fur Company, had visited the Flatheads and left an account of their religious devotion.[8] The Flatheads, no doubt, reflected the religious influence of the Iroquois who had traveled west from the Jesuit Caughnawaga mission at Sault St. Marie in the St. Lawrence Valley. The religious steadfastness of these Iroquois migrants is particularly impressive since they had had no priestly instructions since the Suppression the century before.[9]

As early as 1810 David Thompson employed six Iroquois at Saleesh House near Thompson Falls, in order to assist him in constructing birchbark canoes. These may have settled among the Salish, or returned to Caughnawaga and persuaded others to visit the Bitterroot Valley.[10] Apparently, the leader of the group which settled and intermarried with the Flatheads was Ignace La Mousse (Shonomene), also known as Old Ignace or Ignace the Large to distinguish him from his compatriot of the same name. Along with the others, Ignace had most probably been in the employ of the Hudson's Bay Company until the destruction of the Great League. Having thus traveled from the region of Montreal to Montana, living with the Blackfeet en route, he and the others finally settled with the Flatheads.

Ignace taught the Flatheads to recite the Lord's Prayer, make the sign of the cross and to observe Sun-

---

[8] *Ibid.,* II, p. 238, note 7.

[9] William J. Kip, *Early Jesuit Missions in North America,* provides background information which explains the survival of Catholicism among the Iroquois.

[10] David Thompson, *David Thompson's Narrative of Explorations in Western America, 1784-1812,* ed. by J. B. Tyrrell (Toronto, 1916), p. 418.

day as a day of rest. They did not hunt, fish, trade or move camp on that day. Instead, each Sunday they assembled to listen to the moral teachings of their leader. The service was interspersed with singing and dancing in a great circle after the fashion of the older, native Prophet dance. The remainder of the day was a secular holiday in which the Indians continued to indulge their love of horse racing, the hand game, the ring game, and various other gambling delights.[11]

There is, however, some difference of opinion even among the Catholic missionaries as to the source of the original religious impetus. Father Joseph Joset emphasized the importance of a party of three Indian youths, a Nez Perce, a Spokan and a Coeur d'Alene who traveled to the Red River settlement of the Hudson's Bay Company in 1826. There they received instruction from the Protestant ministers in fundamental Christian teachings. Of the three, Joset added that the Spokan was especially zealous in communicating his new found knowledge and many even of the Coeur d'Alenes were drawn to him.[12] This would explain in part the Nez Perce acceptance of Spalding which Mengarini notes (see "Memorie," Chapter V).

In contrast, at the Kickapoo Mission Father Van Quickenborne by 1836 was keenly aware of the Flatheads' desire to have a Catholic priest. He wrote of this to some unknown correspondent, singling out the number of Christian customs cultivated by these singular tribesmen. "They have asked for a Catholic priest to instruct them in religion," he declared. Again he al-

11 "Apostle of the Iroquois who Brought Faith to Indian," *Montana Catholic Register, West. Ed.* (Helena, Mont.), Aug. 1941.

12 A fuller discussion of this thesis is provided by Drury, *Marcus and Narcissa Whitman,* I, pp. 43-44.

luded to the fact that among them lived a number of
Algonquins and Catholic Iroquois from Canada who
would "like to have their marriages blessed and their
children baptized." [13]

Further support for this account is provided by the
fact that it was Ignace La Mousse who embarked upon
the second expedition in search of the Black Robes. Of
this second expedition, Bishop Rosati later wrote, again
providing some important details. In his account he
explained that after living with the Flatheads for
eighteen years, Ignace La Mousse, called "Le Vieux
Ignace," started for Canada with his two sons in order
to have them baptized. Upon hearing that there were
priests in St. Louis, he altered his course and headed
toward the banks of the Mississippi. The two boys, one
of them only ten years old, were instructed and baptized by the Jesuit Fathers at their college and received
the Christian name of Charles and Francis Xavier.
After receiving absolution, Ignace was assured by
Bishop Rosati that missionaries would be sent to his
people as soon as possible.[14]

Although the traditionally accepted date of this expedition is 1834, an entry in the baptismal record at St.
Louis University establishes the presence of this second
delegation in St. Louis in December 1835. The baptismal register notes: *"2 Decembris Carolus & Xavier-
ius filii legitimi Ignatii, Partus Indiani ex Tribu vulgo
Flatheads solemniter baptizati fuerunt."* [15]

The Flatheads had clearly commissioned Old Ignace to request the services of a Black Robe. But his

[13] Felix Van Quickenbourne to [?], cited in Garraghan, *Jesuits of the Middle United States,* II, p. 239, note 8.

[14] *Ibid.*

[15] Quoted in Mallet, *Origin of the Flathead Mission,* p. 194.

request was not to be immediately fulfilled. Only a promise accompanied him and his sons on their return.

Although Bishop Rosati refers to the death of Ignace La Mousse while on his return trip to the lands of the Flatheads, Ignace, in fact, survived and attempted to lead yet a third delegation to the East.[16] It was on this ill-fated expedition that Old Ignace or Aneas, as he was often called, was killed by Sioux on August 7, 1837.

According to various accounts, the party may have been made up of Old Ignace, three Flatheads and one Nez Perce, or perhaps three Flatheads, one Iroquois and one Snake. In any case, the party reached Ash Hollow, Nebraska, "where they were attacked by three hundred Sioux, and after fighting for three hours killed some fifteen of them." William Gray, a member of the group added that the Sioux dispatched a French trader, Joseph Papier, to negotiate with him and his companions. At the same time they rushed upon "three Flatheads, one Snake and one Iroquois Indian belonging to the party and killed them." [17]

The accuracy of this account is dubious since Big Aneas is first mentioned as being a Flathead and later as an Iroquois guide.[18] Gray also provided a very different version of the fatal ambush and his own escape in narrating the events to Major Peter Ronan. To the Indian agent he explained that he had been "shot in the forehead and exhibited the bullet wound" to Ronan in the winter of 1838. He accounted for his survival by

---

[16] Rosati to Roothaan, cited in Garraghan, *Jesuits of the Middle United States,* II, p. 249.

[17] William Henry Gray, *A History of Oregon, 1792-1849, Drawn from Personal Observations and Authentic Information,* I, p. 173.

[18] Bernard DeVoto, *Across the Wide Missouri,* p. 243, note 24.

explaining that he and his two companions "were kept
in captivity with a view to putting all to death." But
perhaps because the son of the chief had been killed by
Gray, better council prevailed and the Americans were
allowed to depart.[19]

In the summer of 1839, Peter Gaucher (Left-hand
Peter) and Young Ignace embarked upon a fourth ex-
pedition in search of the Black Robes. According to
Flathead tradition, they joined a group of Hudson's
Bay Company men about to make a voyage to St. Louis
by canoe. Their course most naturally lay down the
Yellowstone and Missouri rivers where the two young
suppliants were to have their fortuitous encounter with
Father Pierre Jean De Smet.

Reassured by De Smet's letters of recommendation,
they proceeded to St. Louis and an interview with the
Jesuit Provincial Peter Joseph Verhaegen. Their thrice
repeated request posed a perplexing challenge to the
Jesuits as Verhaegen noted: "Considering the very
great scarcity of priests among us I scarcely knew what
to answer." [20] Finally, after weighing the matter carefully and seeking the opinion of the Consultors, he
promised them that the next spring two Fathers would
undertake the journey to their distant homeland.

Of the fourth delegation, the third to reach St. Louis,
Bishop Rosati wrote: ". . . these savages, who speak
French, have edified us by their truly exemplary con-
duct and interested us by their conversations. The
Fathers of the College have heard their confessions, and

19 Major Peter Ronan, *Historical Sketch of the Flathead Indian Nation from
the Year 1813 to 1890*, p. 26.

20 Verhaegen to Rosati, Nov. 8, 1839, cited in Garraghan, *The Jesuits of
the Middle U.S.*, II, p. 250.

today they approached the holy table at High Mass in the Cathedral and have been confirmed as well." He concluded his report with the observation that one of them would leave the following day to inform the Flatheads that a priest would soon be sent. The other could spend the winter at the mouth of the Bear River and "next spring he will accompany the missionary." [21]

Ironically, the missionary was to be Father De Smet who had first met the travelers at St. Joseph's mission at Council Bluffs. In the company of Young Ignace, his guide, De Smet was to traverse lands largely unknown to white men as he journeyed to the valley of the Bitterroot. In the course of this journey the two finally reached the ragged ridge line of the Rockies. There atop the parapets of the wilderness De Smet celebrated the event in verse. In this scene of solemn loneliness he praised his God and then saluted the immutable "Stonies." In light of days yet to come and travelers yet unborn he wrote:

> All hail majestic Rock – the home
> Where many a wanderer yet shall come;
> Where God himself from his own heart
> Shall health and peace and joy impart.[22]

De Smet's arrival heralded a signal feat. The Jesuits had now breached the heartland of the Northwest, both by land and by sea. Missionaries traveled from Lachine to Vancouver along the Hudson's Bay Company's well-worn routes. Others followed De Smet's trek overland

---

[21] Additional information regarding the four delegations is provided in Chittenden and Richardson, *De Smet*, I, p. 290; Garraghan, *Jesuits of the Middle U.S.*, II, p. 238, notes 7 and 8; Rosati to Roothaan, St. Louis, Oct. 20, 1839, Mt. Sax., GASJ.

[22] Thomas A. Hughes, "The Journal of a Western Missionary," *The Woodstock Letters*, XXI (July 1892), 155.

from Westport along what would become the Oregon Trail. Still others sailed from European ports to the distant Columbia River.[23]

Aware of his role as emissary of Jesuits who would follow, De Smet pressed on to his destination. He crossed the Snake River at the lower end of Jackson's Hole to Teton Pass and into the valley of Pierre's Hole at the foot of the Three Tetons. There he met the main camp of the Flatheads numbering about 1600.[24] A Canadian trader by the name of Brouillet had agreed to join the Indians at the Green River rendezvous in order to assure them that the visitor was indeed a "Black Gown." After seeing De Smet's crucifix, he assured them: "Upon this announcement the chief ordered ten of his warriors to proceed ahead without delay and conduct the missionary to the Flathead camp, the chief following with his whole tribe." [25]

De Smet was escorted to the camp site on the line separating Idaho and Wyoming where the tribesmen soon gathered. After receiving the traditional Flathead greeting, "gest Sgalgat," Chief Big Face offered De Smet his official headdress as a mark of deep friendship.[26] The Jesuit was then conducted to the chief's tent where he was officially welcomed with a speech translated by Gabriel Prudhomme.[27] The recitation was in part thanks and in part a plea: "Kualik (Black Robe), speak! We are all your children. Show us the path

[23] William L. Davis, s.j., *A History of St. Ignatius Mission*, p. 1.

[24] Chittenden and Richardson, *De Smet*, I, pp. 193-94.

[25] Ronan, *Historical Sketch of the Flathead Nation*, p. 27.

[26] "Chief's Authority over Indians Declined by Father P. J. De Smet," *The Sunday Missoulian* (Missoula, Mont.), Aug. 24, 1941, p. 1.

[27] "How the Old Mission of St. Mary's Was Founded," *The Anaconda* (Mont.) *Standard*, Dec. 17, 1899, p. 40.

where abides the Great Spirit. We will follow the words of your mouth." [28]

With the tribe the pioneer priest traveled to Jefferson Fork, arriving at the source of the Missouri River on August 21, 1840.[29] A two-month mission to the Flatheads followed. Religious instructions offered several times a day resulted in the conversion of one hundred and fifty adults and two hundred children. Those brief sixty days also allowed De Smet to develop some plan which he could propose to his co-operator in the "Vineyard of the Lord," the Very Reverend Francis Blanchet. Rather than remain at his post, De Smet planned to go back to St. Louis before winter and return in the spring with a caravan of missionaries. As he explained in a letter to Blanchet: "The *Shoshones* and *Serpents* [Snakes] desire to have an establishment; the *Tetes Plates* and Pend d'Oreilles have nothing more at heart. The Nez Perce seemed to be tired with these self-dubbed ministers *a femmes* and show a great predilection for Catholic priests." [30]

There was much to occupy the missionaries in the mountains, he assured Blanchet, and he fervently hoped to secure a small corps to aid in the task at hand. The field was ripe for harvest; it merely awaited the laborers. That destined band, recruited from Italy, Belgium, France, would soon gather at Westport, on the fringe of American settlement, to assume the challenging task.

---

28 Sister Mary Francesca, "Semi-Centennial of Father De Smet," *The Indian Sentinel,* III (Spring 1923), 53.

29 Edwin V. O'Hara, "De Smet in the Oregon Territory," *Oreg. Hist. Quar.* X (Sept. 1909), 144.

30 De Smet to Blanchet, Fork of Jefferson River, Aug. 10, 1840, quoted in Bagley, *Early Catholic Missions,* p. 97. The missionary referred to is no doubt the Rev. Henry H. Spalding.

The Protestant Response

As Jesuit priests advanced upon a score of missionary fronts, including the disputed Oregon country, a combination of forces also shifted the attention of Americans westward. The period seemed auspicious for advance upon and acquisition of those lands bordering the "Southern Sea." Commerce was becoming a mighty factor along the Great Lakes. Canals and road building pursued at a feverish pace, encouraged by the success of the Erie Canal. Perhaps as a consequence, a contagious spell of wanderlust touched citizens from all parts of the United States. As a result, the ever-moving frontier had pressed out beyond the Blue Grass region of Kentucky into Ohio and Alabama, soon edging its way into lower Illinois. Restless growth pushed pioneers westward toward Missouri along trappers' trails into the disputed lands of Oregon.

By the late 1830s, the dream of a "passage to India" across a united continent had matured into a patriotic axiom. Westerners like Jackson and Clay reminded prospering Americans that their progress would inevitably lead them westward to a wondrous Xanadu. It was "America's manifest destiny!" William Gilpin as well as Senator Thomas Hart Benton and Hall Jackson Kelly avoided no opportunity to remind Americans that before them still lay their "untransacted destiny" to subdue a continent.[1]

As the nineteenth century advanced, Oregon fever was heightened by reports of convenient travel along the Columbia and of favorable markets in the Orient. The productivity of the fertile Willamette Valley made immigration even more enticing. No less was the mood stirred by the idea of a pioneer spirit, "the 'strong bent' of men's spirits, the desire to blaze new trails, to accept a difficult challenge, the thrill of opening a new country, as the lone hunters had done in the Kentucky wilderness."[2]

The westward pursuit of the "star of empire" was also the product of persuasive socio-economic considerations. Increasing waves of foreign settlers, in many cases dislocated by the series of national wars of liberation sweeping across Europe in the 1830s and 1840s, had altered the population pattern along the eastern seaboard, increasing the number of foreign immigrants five-fold in the decade of the 1830s. This influx not only resulted in an "urban press," but also in a potential threat to established cultural patterns. This anxiety fed the nascent forces of "nativism" which would burst into full flower in the Know-Nothingism of the 1850s. A corollary of this apprehension toward foreigners was the growing suspicion of the "popery," to which most immigrant arrivals adhered. News that Catholic missionaries had been sought by the Indians of the Oregon

[1] Henry Nash Smith, *The Virgin Land* (New York, 1950), p. 40.
[2] Ray A. Billington, *Westward Expansion, A History of the American Frontier* (3rd ed.; New York, 1967), p. 52.

Country provided yet another reason for America's vigorous advance upon the Northwest.

In 1833 the Second Provincial Council of the Catholic Church in the United States met at Baltimore. That assembly petitioned Rome to place the care of the Indian missions in the United States under the direction of the Society of Jesus. Rome acceded the following year. The move further aroused anti-Catholic sentiments. In a letter to his sister, Pierre Jean De Smet referred to this tense mood: "It seems that panic has taken possession of the Protestant ministers because of the national council of the bishops of the United States which took place in the month of October last. . . The awful inquisition is about to be established in this beautiful country, the land of liberty."[3]

The vigorous renewal of missionary activity among American Protestants grew not only from a fear that despotic Jesuitism would soon reign over the ruins of traditional Protestantism. The crusade was also inspired by an unprecedented request for missionaries made by an Indian delegation to St. Louis in 1831. The event commanded national attention for it reaffirmed the popular romantic concept of the noble savage.

A sensational account of the visit had been furnished to Gabriel P. Disoway by William Walker, the exploring agent of the Wyandotts. The account appeared in the *Christian Advocate* of New York, the principal organ of the Methodist and Episcopal churches.[4] The

[3] Rev. Pierre Jean De Smet to his sister, Rosalie, St. Louis, Feb. 1, 1830, as quoted in William L. Davis, s.j., "Peter John De Smet, the Years of Preparation, 1801-1837," *Pac. Northwest Quar.* XXXII (Apr. 1941), p. 190; Ray A. Billington, *The Protestant Crusade, 1800-1860* (New York, 1938), pp. 118-41.

[4] New York *Christian Advocate*, Mar. 1, 1833, reprinted in Hiram Chittenden, *The American Fur Trade of the Far West*, II, pp. 894-905.

substance of the account was that a deputation of Flathead chiefs had come in search of the "true god" about
whom they had heard from an adventurer attending one
of their feasts. He had told them of the Great Book
which contained the wisdom of the "Great Spirit." [5] It
was to their friend General William Clark, Superintendent of Indian Affairs, that they turned in St. Louis. [6]

The American mentality was more than receptive to
the inspired entreaty of the delegation. Church groups,
not yet rent by sectionalism and the issue of slavery,
eagerly responded. Lyman Beecher toured the East
with his "Plea for the West," and the *American
Protestant Vindicator* urged the formation of Flathead
societies.

The response was phenomenal. Flathead societies
sprang up as far away as Connecticut. Upon reading
the account, Wilbur Fiske, president of Wesleyan University, was visibly moved as he read the account of the
"four flat Head Indians" to his wife. Next day he began
to collect funds for the mission. As a result, his wife
wrote to a friend, $700 to $800 were raised "in our small
city to assist in its [the mission's] outfit." [7]

Before the arrival of the Indian delegation in St.
Louis, efforts at Christian conversion of the Indians had
been limited to those residing at Hudson's Bay settlements. As early as 1825, the Reverend David T. Jones

---

[5] Attributed to these Indians is an eloquent oration delivered at a banquet
before their departure in which one of the Flatheads expressed his disappointment at not securing the coveted book. Garraghan, *Jesuits of the Middle U.S.*,
II, p. 244.

[6] Often referred to as the "Flathead Delegation," there is continuing discussion as to its actual composition. The various possible combinations are
examined by Garraghan, *Jesuits of the Middle U.S.*, II, p. 243, note 19. See
also Clifford M. Drury, *Marcus and Narcissa Whitman*, I, pp. 37-49.

[7] Wade C. Barcley, *History of the Methodist Missions*, II, p. 200.

persuaded Governor George Simpson to send two Spokan Indian youths to the Red River settlement. To one
was given the name "Spokan Garry" and to the other,
"Kootenay Pelly." In the summer of 1829 they returned
to their tribe. Such was their enthusiasm that five more
joined them in 1830. There Pelly died the following
year. Correspondence between Dr. John McLoughlin
and Simon McGillivray suggests that by this time
Spokan Garry had been preaching among the tribes of
the Upper Columbia for some months.[8]

These initial efforts multiplied as the plight of the
pious Flatheads galvanized Protestant evangelism.
Within months after publication of the Disoway letter,
the buckskin successors of the frontier circuit riders
sought out the upper reaches of the Missouri River.
Perhaps the earliest Christian missionary to preach in
what is now Montana and Idaho was the Reverend
Samuel Parker of the Congregational Church of Mid-
dlefield, Massachusetts.[9] After reading the 1833 account
of the Indian delegation in the *Christian Advocate,* he
promptly decided to pursue a missionary life.

In September 1834, Jason and Daniel Lee with a
party of Methodists also answered the call. This group
eventually settled in Oregon, Jason Lee at a mission in
the Willamette Valley, and Daniel Lee along with two
lay brothers at the Dalles or Narrows along the Columbia River. By 1841 other Methodist missions had been
established among the Chinooks at the mouth of the

---

[8] For a more complete account of these events, consult Thomas E. Jessett,
Spokan Garry; Clifford M. Drury, "Oregon Indians of the Red River School,"
Pac. Hist. Rev., XXIX (Mar. 1938), 50-60; Mengarini, "Memorie," Chapter v,
herein.

[9] Stanley Davison, "Worker in God's Wilderness," *Montana Magazine of
Western History,* VII (Jan. 1957), pp. 8-17.

Columbia. An attempt to establish yet another among the Nisqually Indians near Puget Sound foundered when the Indians disappeared.[10]

The formal initiation of missionary work among the Indians, however, was sponsored by the American Board of Commissioners for Foreign Missions, supported by the Congregational, Presbyterian, and Dutch Reform churches. Promptly heeding the "Macedonian Cry" from the Indians of Oregon, it dispatched a party consisting of the Rev. Henry Harmon Spalding and his recent bride Eliza, and Dr. Marcus Whitman, a physician and catechist who had been sent on an initial expedition with Parker the year before, and his bride Narcissa. Along with William H. Gray, a mechanic, and two Indian youths Whitman had befriended on a reconnaissance of the area the year before, the group set out in 1836 to establish missions among the Flathead and the Nez Perce.[11]

Part of the company settled near Fort Walla Walla where the energetic Whitman, with the aid of Mr. Gray, built a station at Waiilatpu on the Walla Walla River and established the first Presbyterian Church in North America west of the Rockies.[12] Work also progressed at the Rev. Spalding's mission station at Lapwai near Clearwater.[13] By 1838 the number of workers had

---

[10] Robert H. Blossom, "First Presbyterian on the Pacific Coast," *Oreg. Hist. Quar.,* xv (June 1914), pp. 81-103; George H. Himes, "Beginnings of Christianity in Oregon," *Oreg. Hist. Quar.* xx (June 1919), pp. 159-79; Joseph Williams, *Narrative of a Tour from the State of Indiana to the Oregon in the Years 1841-42,* pp. 26-27.

[11] A comprehensive account of this enterprise is provided in Drury's *Marcus and Narcissa Whitman,* and in Clifford M. Drury, ed., *First White Women over the Rockies.*

[12] Blossom, "First Presbyterians on the Pacific," p. 84.

[13] Bagley, *Early Catholic Missions,* pp. 54-55.

increased as reinforcements arrived. With the group came the Reverends Cushing Eells and Elkanah Walker. The arrival increased the size of the vanguard Presbyterian congregation which consisted of

> . . . six charter members including Joseph Maki and his wife Maria, Hawaiians in Whitman's employ, Charles Compo a mountain man, as well as the two Whitmans and Mrs. Spalding. As pastor Spalding was excluded. . . also included were twenty Nez Perce and one Cayuse convert.[14]

Soon the major thrust of work seemed directed toward the organization of the white settlers. On May 25, 1844, "The Presbyterian Church of Willamette Falls" was formed. On September 19, 1846, Lewis Thompson organized another at Clatsop Plains south of Astoria.[15] Settlements at Salem and Oregon City followed. Clearly, the focus of the Protestant missioners had shifted toward the white settlers. In growing numbers, pioneers were crossing the Rockies and settling in the valley of Oregon. The more stable these settlements, the more firm became the United States' claim to the land which was disputed by Great Britain.

Underlying this turning away from the native Indians was yet another reason. Throughout the Protestant missionary ranks there was a general frustration with their program of religious instruction of the Indians. In 1839 the first printing press had arrived. The next year was spent translating and printing portions of the Bible and school books for Indian use. But of this first printing done in the Oregon Territory, the Rev. Spalding was to observe in dismay: "Every verb

---

[14] Clifford M. Drury, "Some Aspects of Presbyterian History in Oregon," *Oreg. Hist. Quar.,* LVC (June 1954), pp. 145-59.

[15] *Ibid.,* p. 146.

seems to be endless in its conjugations and combinations.
I have carried an active transitive verb through several
thousand forms." [16]

The frustration was compounded by the evident
progress of the Catholic missionaries who found the
Indians remarkably teachable. More impulsive writers
attributed the success of the Catholics to the fact that
their rituals appealed to the savage mind. One added,
"Heathenish superstitions and idolotry produce a state
of mind and heart well fitted to give credence to papal
superstition and idolotry." [17]

The problem of educating the Indians also beset
Cushing Eells. Writing in the *Missionary Herald,* February 25, 1840, he noted: "I cannot learn that they have
any realizing of the odiousness of sin. . . They do
not lack the ability to learn, but rather the inclina-
tion." [18]

Aware of this tendency, Jason Lee emphasized the
material arts of civilization, and called his mission
establishment the "Methodist Oregon Mission Indian
Manual Labor School." [19] The Indians east of the Cas-
cades were supposedly decidedly inferior to the Sali-
shans. Since churches in the East continued to send
funds, Lee simply modified his program to their needs.

The frustrations felt by Spalding and Eells soon
paled with the massacre of fourteen of Dr. Whitman's
group at the Waiilatpu mission in 1847. The imme-

---

[16] Read Bain, "Educational Plans and Efforts by Methodists in Oregon to
1860," *Oreg. Hist. Quar.,* XXI (Mar. 1920), pp. 63-94.

[17] Robert F. Berkhofer, Jr., *Salvation and the Savage, an Analysis of
Protestant Missions and American Indian Response, 1787-1862,* p. 95.

[18] Bain, "Educational Plans of Methodists," p. 68.

[19] *Ibid.,* p. 69.

diate explanation for the atrocity appeared to be Indian suspicion of Dr. Whitman's intentions in treating the natives during a measles epidemic. Some believed that in an effort to secure Indian land, Whitman had poisoned them.[20] The fact that this violence was accompanied by trouble at Spalding's Lapwai mission, and that during that same year, 1847, Mengarini reported prolonged and open dissension at St. Mary's, suggests a more generalized basis for aggression. The exploitation, the double standards of morality exhibited by white settlers, and most of all, the loss of identity the Indian sensed as he was overwhelmed by the advancing white culture, led to these antipathies. The result was violence, or capitulation, or even withdrawal to primitivism reflected in the Smohalla movement a decade later.[21]

Rather than joyfully rejoining the lost sheep with the flock, the missionary, both Protestant and Catholic, had served as harbinger of a socio-economic and cultural system painfully alien to the Indians' own.

[20] Drury, *Marcus and Narcissa Whitman,* II, pp. 211-12.
[21] Richard Forbis, "Religious Acculturation Among the Flathead Indians" (Unpublished Master's thesis, Mont. St. Univ., 1950), p. 23.

ST. MARY'S MISSION CHAPEL
The chapel after restoration in Stevensville, Montana.

FATHER PIERRE JEAN DeSMET
DeSmet was the first Black Robe to directly contact the Flatheads.
Courtesy, Jesuit Historical Archives, Crosby Lby., Gonzaga Univ.

On the Trail

While the American Board missionaries labored in the Oregon country, Father Pierre Jean De Smet freely pursued his own missionary dream. He found the zeal of the Flatheads was even more fervent than reported. After baptizing three hundred fifty, he decided to return to St. Louis in order to raise funds and gather men to expand the mission. He could then return to properly tend his "vineyard ripe for harvest." With a visionary's impatience he again climbed the precipitous "Stonies" and traversed the seemingly endless prairie before reaching St. Louis. From there he journeyed to Philadelphia to request that a general collection be conducted throughout the diocese in support of his program. Again in New Orleans additional funds were raised.[1]

Thus with over one thousand dollars, a supply of useful articles, and official designation as Superior of the Rocky Mountain missions by Father Verhaegen, De Smet began to organize for the return to the Bitterroot Valley. But first it was necessary to gather pro-

[1] Chittenden and Richardson, *De Smet*, I, p. 274.

visions, firearms and wagons, including four carts and an ox-drawn wagon which was to be the first ever to reach Montana.[2] Most important of all was the selection of guides and an experienced caravan captain to lead the band over more than eight hundred leagues of land to be traversed. Ahead lay six to eight months of distressful journeying across the uncharted wilderness.[3]

At length, on April 24, 1841, De Smet departed in the company of Fathers Gregory Mengarini and Anthony Eysvogels, the latter assigned to the Potawatomi mission of St. Joseph. Traveling with them were Brothers Huet, Specht and Claessens. On the day they finally left St. Louis, Mengarini wrote to Father General Roothaan: "The Caravan has been found and today, April 24 . . . we are setting out for Westport where we shall find Fr. Point and thence proceed to the Rocky Mountains."[4]

As the steamer *Oceana* pulled away from the dock for the seven-day journey up the Missouri River, many were the glances cast toward this group of foreign religious: twenty-nine-year-old William Claessens, the Belgian blacksmith; thirty-five-year-old Charles Huet, a carpenter also from Belgium; and the German, Joseph Specht, a tinner and factotem. With the Brothers was the newly ordained Gregory Mengarini, an Italian, who although only twenty-nine, had been selected by the Father General himself because of his virtues, his great facility with languages, and his knowledge of medicine and music.[5]

---

[2] Wilfred A. Schoenberg, *Jesuits in Montana* (Portland, 1960), p. 13.

[3] Garraghan, *Jesuits of the Middle U.S.*, II, p. 256.

[4] Mengarini to Fr. Gen. John Roothaan, s.j., St. Louis, Apr. 24, 1841, Mt. Sax. [illegible citation], GASJ.

[5] Chittenden and Richardson, *De Smet*, I, p. 278.

At a camp not far from the shore of the Kaw River near the Sapling Grove rendezvous, the missionary party was joined by what was to be the first wagon train of emigrants to the Pacific Coast. According to John Bidwell, a member of the party, the sixty-four overland pioneers joined De Smet's small group of seventeen.[6] At this point De Smet had secured the assistance of Thomas "Broken Hand" Fitzpatrick as guide, a man whom Bidwell soon described as pilot of the whole "tho he had never been across the continent, but had been a hunter and trapper in the neighborhood of the headwaters of the Columbia."[7]

On May 10, the combined groups departed from Westport. Wagon wheels rolled along the trail leading to the Platte River. Within a week before leaving Sapling Grove, the group which had joined the Jesuits was organized into a company. Serving as secretary was "young John Bidwell — recently a school teacher in Platte County, Mo. . . John Bartleson (aged fifty-four, of Jackson County, Mo.) was elected Captain."[8]

Fortunately, the progress of the caravan was recorded by several members, including the missionaries' official diarist, Father Point. Of the overland life he wrote: "The duties of the guide [Fitzpatrick] were very important; thus, the Captain at early dawn gave the signal

[6] A more detailed description of the party that was organized is offered by Nunis, *Belden*, pp. 126-36; John Bidwell, "The First Immigrant Train to California," *The Century Illustrated Monthly Magazine*, XLI (Nov. 1890), pp. 106-30; LeRoy Hafen and William J. Ghent, *Broken Hand, the Life Story of Thomas Fitzpatrick, Chief of the Mountain Men* (Denver, 1930), pp. 127-34; Chittenden and Richardson, *De Smet*, I, pp. 272-314; Williams, *Narrative of a Tour*, pp. 1-18.

[7] Nunis, *Belden*, p. 37.

[8] Barry, "Annals of Kansas," p. 346. For a detailed discussion of the number and the members of the company, see Nunis, *Belden*, pp. 126-36.

for rising and for departure and once upon the road he regulated the march and halting times; he also chose the ground for camp and looked to keeping discipline."

Of the care taken against attacks from hostile Indians, Point adds that for greater security each owner tied his stock to stakes which were long enough to permit grazing. Even with these precautions, however, Point writes, "From the first moment sleep reigned over the camp until the following daybreak" each traveler including the priests kept watch.[9]

Father Point goes on to observe that the party used a variety of precautions in travel. Particularly deliberate preparations preceded the fording of rivers. "Whilst the first driver goaded them on from his high seat," his subordinates shouted and whipped the team to make it advance. To preclude any loss, things were kept well-balanced with safety cords stretched across the tops of the wagons. Nevertheless Point's calm was assailed by "the roaring waters, the bellowing of the oxen and the neighing of the horses, and the excited shouts of the drivers." All combined to make "the most horrid din I ever listened to." He concludes, "It was astonishing that we effected the passage without mishap."[10]

An artist of considerable sensitivity, Point gazed with rapture upon the limitless expanse of the Great Prairie and with unrestrained curiosity upon the Delaware and Shawnee encampments as the party trudged and strained toward the banks of the Kansas. There two

---

[9] Nicolas Point, s.J., "Recollections of the Rocky Mountain Missions," *The Woodstock Letters*, XI (1882), p. 6.

[10] *Ibid.*, p. 7.

more members who had taken baggage upriver in a pirogue joined them at a crossing near Topeka.[11]

Of the company of twenty wagons, carrying seventy-seven people, fifty men were capable of managing a rifle. The number grew as stragglers joined, the last of whom was Joseph Williams, a Protestant minister from Indiana, who De Smet described as a man of "ingenious simplicity." [12] Williams noted De Smet's kindness, but also revealed a certain self-righteous anger in describing the company in his *Narrative:* "There were some as wicked people as I ever saw in all my life. . . Our leader, Fitzpatrick, is a wicked, worldly man and is much opposed to missionaries going among the Indians." [13]

The sun rose and the sun set, but the end of the journey was still over a thousand miles away, mused the disconsolate and saddle-weary Mengarini. Sometimes John Grey, a hunter and trapper for the party would say to him in the morning, "Father, do you see that speck in the distance? Today we must reach there." The weary missionary would hopefully reply, "Then our day's journey will be short." To this the hunter would laughingly reply, "We shall see." The hours of the morning would pass and the company would usually have journeyed long under the scorching afternoon sun "before the speck would assume appreciable magnitude and distinctness of form." Disappointedly, Mengarini

[11] Point, *Wilderness Kingdom,* p. 26.

[12] Chittenden and Richardson, *De Smet,* I, p. 297.

[13] It is worthy of note that at no point in the narrative does Joseph Williams refer to the members of the Jesuit missionary party, brothers or priests, with the exception of De Smet who kindly offered him a serving of venison soon after their meeting. *Narrative,* p. 809.

admitted "that the last rays of the setting sun would often show us, still miles distant, the welcomed grove where we would find water and rest." [14]

In the same narrative Mengarini describes an occasion when Grey was forced to search for a ford. Having found one, he started across with others close behind. Some felt they could find a better way for themselves "and so scattered after entering the river," leaving the guide's path muddled and uncertain. For safety's sake Mengarini determined to follow the wagon ahead of him, but as both neared the other bank, the wagon toppled and Mengarini felt "the earth slipping from beneathe my horse's feet." "If not gracefully, at least firmly," he clung to the horse's neck for, since he could not swim, he "held on to life more vigorously," he later explained. Although the current was strong, the horse saved himself and his rider, and within minutes the two struggled to the bank while the abandoned wagon floated downstream. The abashed tenderfoot "retired quite a distance" and hung up his clothes to dry. Comfortable once more the Reverend Father returned to camp only to be reminded that while clinging frantically to the neck of his horse, it was difficult to distinguish him from his steed. [15]

The missionaries and their party traveled with the vanguard. Each day the captain, known to most Indian tribes as *Tête Blanch* (White Head), would give the signal to rise, and plan the march, choosing the stops to make camp. Upon reaching the campsite the company would be arranged in the pattern of a circle or a square to provide a secure, enclosed grazing area for the

---

[14] Partoll, "Mengarini's Narrative," pp. 194-95.
[15] *Ibid.*

animals. From the moment camp was made until sunrise, all the company with the exception of Fitzpatrick and De Smet, stood watch.[16]

A small change in the routine occurred on May 19. "Father De Smet and Father Point bore off to the left to visit the first village of Kansa," numbering about seven or eight hundred.[17] Artist Point noted especially the strong character written on the faces of these Indians, the vivacity of expression, singularity of dress, and their close resemblance to the neighboring Osage, while they in turn marvelled at Father Point's bearded face since a beardless chin and well-picked brows and eyelashes were considered by them indispensable criteria of Indian beauty.

The endless trek across the wilderness trail was marked by another notable event ten days later. On the afternoon of Saturday, May 29, the company discerned a waterspout swirling along the horizon. As it struck the river, it generated a billowing foam, and swept over the land wreaking the vengeance of the dreaded tornado. Presently, the trees on the river bank swayed violently. Some were torn from their roots and "a great mist, spreading rapidly over the river, discharged itself in a fall of hail." The party dismounted until the shower passed. Then starting forward again, Father Point spied, "partially embedded in the soil, something that seemed to be a beautiful piece of quartz, oval in shape and about the size of a goose egg." He hastened to pick it up and found to his astonishment that it was a hail stone.[18]

[16] Point, *Wilderness Kingdom*, p. 26.

[17] *Ibid.*, p. 27.

[18] Partoll, "Mengarini's Narrative," p. 194.

As they traveled the lone pioneers sometimes fell in with bands of Sioux and Cheyennes, but no harm ever befell them. Often they were without water. Often the road was lost. "But why speak of road," Mengarini complained, "when no such thing existed! Plains on all sides. 'Plains at morning; plains at noon; plains at night.' And this, day after day." [19]

By the end of May the prairies gave way to higher bluffs bordering the Platte River. Here the travelers met the first buffalo as they passed six flatbottom boats loaded with hides floating down the shallow Platte. Soon the surrounding plains were covered with buffalo bones and skulls. Within a few more days, while traveling up the north side of the South Fork, the group saw a herd of thousands of buffalo. [20]

Thus far that journey had been relatively calm, but between Grand Island and Green River (reached July 23) a number of events occurred, "including two weddings, one death [James Shotwell] by accident, some 'desertions,' a few accessions [a company of trappers under command of Henry Fraeb] and Nicholas Dawson's encounter with Indians." [21]

May, June, July had scorched their pathway when the group finally parted. By August 15 the party reached Fort Hall in southern Idaho. [22] Here, De Smet

[19] Mengarini explains that such were the hardships that potable water was converted from putrid stagnant water found in hollows, while prairie hens, prairie cocks, and antelopes supplied needed food. *Ibid.*, p. 195.

[20] Williams, *Narrative*, p. 11.

[21] Barry, "Annals of Kansas," p. 347. Belden adds that the Cheyenne returned Dawson's gun and pistol upon request. Demonstrating no more hostility, they traded a bit for tobacco and beads. Nunis, *Belden*, p. 39.

[22] Fort Hall was under the official direction of the Chief Factor of the Hudson's Bay Company, Dr. John McLoughlin. In a letter dated Sept. 27, 1841, he offered assistance and advice to the missionary group, noting: "And [as] our

left and journeyed ahead with a small group of Flatheads who had met him the day before.

In a letter from Fort Hall De Smet observed that the
reunion with the Flatheads had occurred on the eve of
the feast of the Assumption. Its joy he saw reflected "in
the beaming serenity" of the neophytes and the "feeling
manner in which they pressed our hands." He continued to marvel at what they had done to secure the
ministry of the "Black Gowns." For twenty years "in
compliance with the counsels of the poor Iroquois .
. . they had conformed as nearly as they could, to
our creed, our manners, and De Smet adds "even to our
religious ceremonials." He concluded his praise by
recalling that in the preceding ten years "four deputations . . . had courageously ventured to St. Louis,
over a space of 3,000 miles – over mountains and valleys
infested by Blackfeet and other hostile tribes." [23]

The fulfillment of an ardent request was reason
enough for jubilation. The main camp awaited De
Smet's arrival while Gabriel Prudhomme, the two sons
of old Ignace, young Pelchimo, and old Simon Peter,
the most elderly of the tribe and the one baptized by
De Smet on his previous visit, escorted the welcome
newcomer to their camp site. Once astride their horses,
old Simon who even when seated needed a stick to support himself, announced to the young warriors: "My
children, I shall accompany you; If I die on the way,
our Fathers at least, will know the cause of my death!"
With whip in hand it was old Simon Peter who urged

means of conveyance are not always at command, it would be necessary you
sent us your list of demands in the month of January for what you required
in June and in the month of July for what you may require in fall and
winter." McLoughlin to De Smet, Vancouver, Sept. 27, 1841. Mt. Sax., GASJ.

[23] Reuben Gold Thwaites, ed., *Early Western Travels,* XXVII, p. 229.

his youthful followers forward at the rate of fifty miles a day.[24]

The main camp had awaited De Smet's arrival between July 1 and July 16 at a point agreed upon along the Wind River. As provisions diminished, however, the Flatheads had been forced to temporarily withdraw into the mountains. From his interpreter, Prudhomme, De Smet also learned that "the whole tribe had determined to fix upon some spot a site for a permanent village; that, with this in view, they had already chosen two places which they believed to be suitable, that nothing but our presence was required to confirm their determination. . ."[25] The little band traveled north from Fort Hall until it reached the Beaverhead River in southwestern Montana. There the group met the rest of the tribe, who warmly greeted De Smet. On September 9, the last stage of the Jesuits' journey began. Accompanied by the Flatheads they moved toward the Hell Gate defile. "If the road to the infernal regions," wrote Father Mengarini, "were as uninviting as that of its namesake, few I think would care to travel it."[26]

Down the steep trails lurched the first wagons to cross western Montana. Along precarious ledges the precious cargo swayed as hostile Indians, including the Bannocks, spied at a distance. Though De Smet was delighted at the prospect of meeting new tribes, Mengarini, "like a bishop donning robes and clutching his mitre, hastily put on his cassock. When asked where his gun was he confidently displayed his reliquary."[27]

---

[24] Chittenden and Richardson, *De Smet*, I, p. 291.
[25] *Ibid.*, I, p. 293.
[26] Schoenberg, *Jesuits in Montana,* p. 13.
[27] *Ibid.*

Having descended to the prairie below, the group followed the Hell Gate River to which the Fathers gave the name St. Ignatius. Along its banks they camped for several days, making short scouting trips in search of a suitable place for a permanent mission. Finally, they decided upon a site in the middle of the valley on the bank of the Bitterroot, a tributary of the Flathead or the Clark River which flows in a northwesterly direction until it reaches the Columbia.[28] There on September 24, 1841, the feast of Our Lady of Mercy, the Jesuits unhitched their squeaking carts. To cap the victorious climax to this harrowing trek, the brother-cook found that the Jesuits' food supplies were completely exhausted. It was Mengarini who piously replied: "God will provide. Wait!" That afternoon the Indians began to arrive with a load of buffalo meat. "Did I not tell you?" cried Mengarini triumphantly.[29]

As the faithful Indians left their offerings, they gathered around a large wooden cross De Smet had erected. All, from chief to youngest child, came forth to press their lips against it while others chanted the "Vexilla Regis." The Society now claimed a new citadel dedicated "to the greater glory of God."

[28] Mallet, "Origin of the Flathead Mission," p. 204.
[29] Schoenberg, *Jesuits in Montana*, p. 13.

GREGORY MENGARINI

The Man of Two Worlds

The arduous journey to the land of the Flatheads had been successfully completed. Now the organization of the mission station ensued. By St. Martin's day on the first Sunday of October 1841, the rude house and chapel were built, and the mission was formally dedicated. During that same month representatives from twenty-four neighboring Indian nations came to visit the Black Robes. By November, after their return from the hunt, one-third of the Flatheads had been baptized. The energizing force behind this progress was the young pastor of St. Mary's, a scholar, surely unsettled by the rudeness of the frontier, but long committed to fulfilling his destiny in this new land.

Gregory Mengarini had been born into a distinguished, aristocratic Roman family on the feast of St. Ignatius, July 21, 1811.[1] In October of his seventeenth year he began preparation for eventual ordination in the Society of Jesus. During his scholasticate he served as instructor in grammar at Rome, Modena and Reg-

[1] Allen Johnson and Dumas Malone, eds., *Dictionary of American Biography* (21 vols.; New York, 1937-1945), XII, p. 535.

gio. It was during this period that his particularly acute
philological bent became evident.[2]

During his second year of theology, the young Jesuit
heard read in the refectory of the Roman College
Bishop Rosati's account of the first Flathead delegation
to St. Louis. This seemingly ingenuous act of faith filled
him with admiration. His life's work was decided! He
would prepare himself to minister to the Indians of the
Rocky Mountains.[3] In a letter to his Father Provincial,
December 25, 1839, he explained that this desire had
been born within him fifteen years before when he had
first decided to join the Society. Each of the eleven
years since his entry, he added, he had implored of
"St. Francis Xavier the grace to pursue what one might
call this second vocation from God." He concluded:
"I request of Your Paternity, assignment to the foreign
missions and if you should ask where, I would answer
any place."[4]

Within him, however, grew the secret hope that he
would be assigned to the North American missions
after his ordination in 1840.[5] After subjecting himself
to trial after trial in an effort to prove and test the
sincerity of his vocation, both he and his superiors were
convinced of his tenacity and zeal and he was granted
permission to embark for the United States in the company of Father James Cotting.[6] Mengarini and his

2 *The Catholic Encyclopedia* (15 vols.; New York, 1911), X, pp. 188-89.
This need for linguistic talent was also stressed by Fidel Grivel in Hughes,
History, II, p. 1010.

3 William N. Bischoff, *Jesuits in Old Oregon, A Sketch of Jesuit Activities
in the Pacific Northwest, 1840-1940* (Caldwell, Id., 1945), p. 28.

4 Gregory Mengarini to Rev. Fr. Gen. John Roothaan, S.J., Rome, Dec. 25,
1839, Mt. Sax., GASJ. Consult App. A.

5 *Enciclopedia Italiana* (36 vols.; Rome, 1934), XXII, p. 854.

6 "Father Mengarini," *The Woodstock Letters*, XVI (1887), p. 93.

companion rushed to Leghorn impetuously convinced that a mere estuary separated them from their field of labor. His eagerness was to no avail. From June 21 until July 23, the young evangelists waited to board the *Oriole*.[7] Mengarini had hastened through his theology examinations in order to be ordained in advance in March 1840. He had breathlessly bid farewell – forever – to friends and family only to stare, it seemed, at a silent ship eternally anchored in port.

Once on the high seas the two passed additional weary weeks hopelessly scanning the horizon for some outline of the port of Philadelphia. To tediousness was added turbulence. A storm had arisen on the Atlantic and the usual three weeks allowed for the crossing lengthened to eight. Though the tempest eventually passed, the wind still blew a gale. Provisions grew scarce, though a "few inches" of dried sausage was offered by a passing vessel. Consequently, Mengarini's seafarer's palate developed perforce a tolerance for sea tortoise, shark and dolphin. Not so for poor Cotting. For him seasickness became the order of the day.[8]

The landing in the city of "brotherly love" was no more cheerful. Despite Mengarini's general facility with language, few understood the two. Furthermore, the expenses were unexpectedly high, and the complications of travel caused some embarrassment to the two as they traveled from Baltimore to Georgetown. In later years Mengarini recalled with chagrin his first evening train ride in the United States. The locomotive appeared to streak through the darkness and then quite suddenly stop. Whereupon Mengarini noted, "the fel-

[7] Mengarini, "Rocky Mountains," p. 298.
[8] *Ibid.*, p. 300.

low-passengers rose from their seats and went out .
. ." Whither the foreign arrivals did not know. To
their astonishment Cotting and Mengarini discovered
the travelers hastily eating at nearby tables.

"Come," said Mengarini, "let us follow their example." Cotting hesitated, and as he finally sat down,
protested, "It is all a speculation." No sooner had the
two been seated, but a noise was heard, marking the
departure of the others who vanished into the darkness.
"Just before the lights were put out," Mengarini wrote,
"we saw a lady and a gentleman walking near us." Mengarini, the accomplished linguist asked, *"Parlez-vous
Francais?"* But the two passed on after replying with
an abrupt, *"Pas beaucoup."*

The confused duo could do nothing but pray. Moments later their appeal was answered, Mengarini
explained. "Suddenly we heard a noise of shouting. The
lights which had been going farther and farther, seemed
now to be coming nearer and nearer." A man muttering
unintelligibly, the priest added, "dragged us after him
aboard another train." The two young men found themselves dazzled with light and unable to conceal their
embarrassment as they learned "it had been necessary
. . . to cross a river and change cars" to continue
their journey. Only their guardian angels and the station master had saved them from abandonment.[9]

There is a seed of the heroic in all men, and each is
tempted to reach beyond the familiar to create something unique, and perhaps more exalted than he has
known. No doubt, at this point the Jesuit missionaries
questioned the prudence of their own heroic vision.
Certainly, Mengarini, a man of birth and position, must

[9] *Ibid.,* pp. 300-01.

FATHER GREGORY MENGARINI
Courtesy, Jesuit Historical Archives, Crosby Lby., Gonzaga Univ.

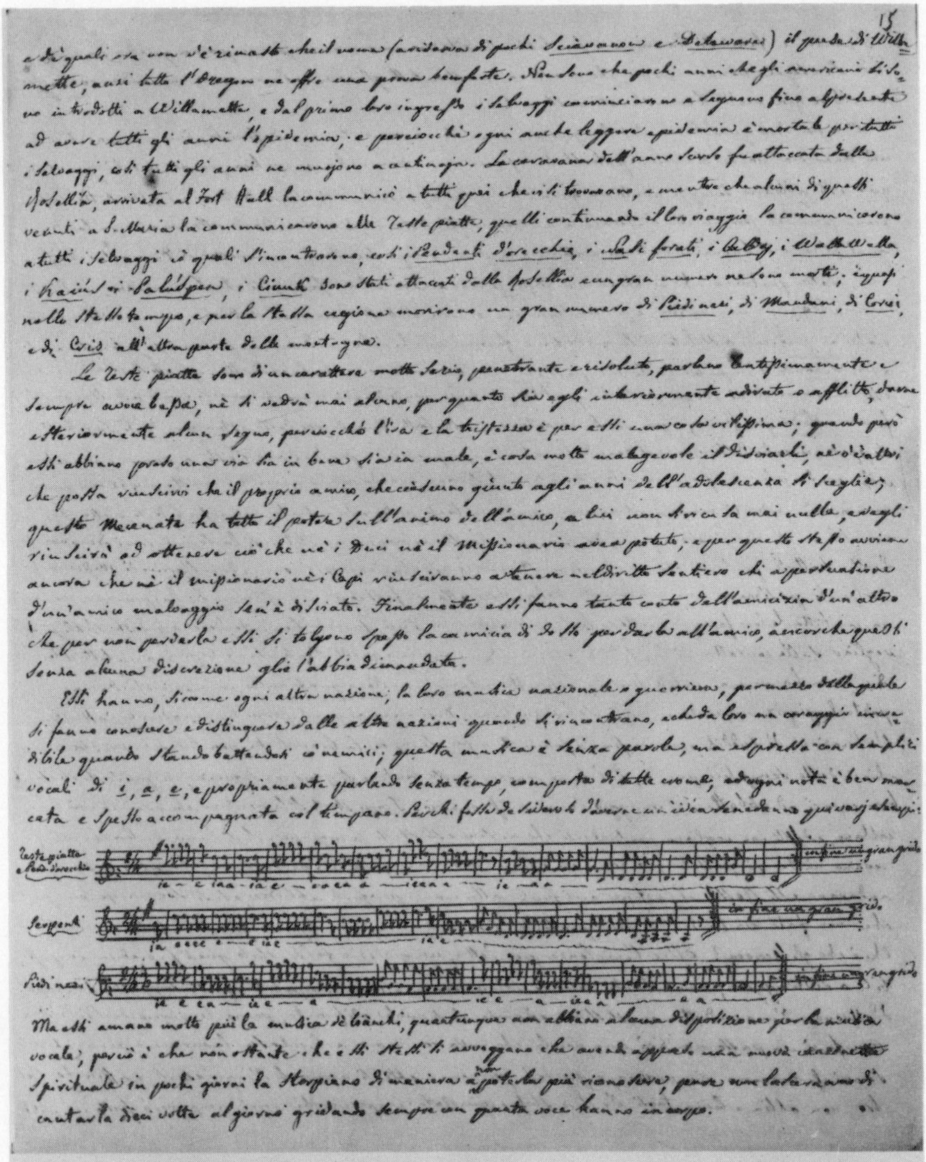

A Page from the Document

A page of the *Memorie* in Mengarini's hand. *See* page 200.

From the author's microfilm copy of the manuscript.

have reflected upon the forces which were leading him to Georgetown and on across the continent in pursuit of the "wigwams of Idaho." The justifications for his choice were many. First of all, from the days of the Genoese traders, Italians had traditionally explored the outer limits of civilization – on the Guinea Coast, in Peiping and even earlier, in the Levant.

Furthermore, the political unrest which beset a fragmented Italy attempting to anneal itself into a nation state had peopled the new world with disillusioned Italian exiles.[10] The brief Napoleonic occupation had only served to humiliate, not unite Italians.

Those who had survived the arbitrary partition of the "geographic expression" its citizens dared call Italy, witnessed the famines, epidemics and commercial stagnation which followed the Congress of Vienna. They paid the increasing taxes which rendered truthless the Italian aphorism, *"chi ha pratto ha tutto"* (who has land has everything).[11] Inevitably, these factors in combination with such realities as a population density of one hundred and thirteen persons per square mile by the end of the century, led to a psychology of deprivation.[12] In contrast to the poverty of *il Mezzogiorno* (in the south), early Italian immigrants wrote of the vastness of wealth of America's interior land mass. In fact, in 1889, it was an Italian, Achille Loria, who pointed to free, unoccupied land as a source of economic growth – a theory that by Frederick Jackson

---

[10] William L. Langer, comp., *Encyclopedia of World History* (3rd rev. ed.; Cambridge, Mass., 1962), p. 650.

[11] Andrew Rolle, *Immigrant Upraised, Italian Adventurers and Colonists in Expanding America* (Norman, Okla., 1968), p. 20.

[12] This same point is dealt with at length by Luigi Barzini, *The Italians* (New York, 1964), pp. 106-21.

Turner's admission was to mold our own historical concept of the frontier.

Such was the promise of the American myth. Coupled with the entreaties of the "noble savage," frontier America became as irresistible to the patrician Roman Mengarini as it had been to the Bostonian Francis Parkman. Furthermore, to the sensuality and primitivism inherent in nineteenth century Romanticism, Allesandro Manzoni, father of Italian Romanticism, had added an ardent Catholicism.[13] The spirit of St. Francis Xavier, of St. Thomas the Apostle, or Isaac Jogues epitomized the romantic idealism of the age and helped galvanize Mengarini's youthful enthusiasm for the unspoiled simplicity of the "savages" of the Rockies.

There was, however, another factor which may have significantly contributed to Mengarini's decision. After Napoleon's first onslaught, Italy had been divided yet again. The Union of Upper Italy under Eugene Beauharnais and in the south under Joseph Bonaparte cynically offered the traditionally subject Italian only ineluctable hope of union from Alps to the sea.[14] The sacking of Italian treasures by Napoleon, the devious manipulation of the Papacy, and the conditions stipulated by Campo Formio further served to shame a proud people.

The carcass of Italy thus rendered at Metternich's "abattoir" of Vienna, which had publicly pledged a return to the *status quo,* resulted in a continuing despotism. As a result there grew within them either embittered cynicism, or generous idealism.

---

13 Evelyn Cesanesco, *Liberation of Italy, 1815-1870* (London, 1895), p. 20.
14 *Ibid.,* p. 12.

At the embattled center of a fragmented Italy the restored papacy of Pius VII had sufficient dragoons, grenadiers and artillery to maintain tranquility.[15] Thus the Carbonari uprisings of 1821 resulted in widespread imprisonment and in 1823 nationalist agitators were confined to the horrible prisons of the Papal States. Under Austrian influence the suppression did not relent with the accession of Leo XII. Yet within the next two years Giovanni Mazzini's Young Italy organization moved upon the Papal States.

Against this setting of frustrated nationalism and youthful idealism Gregory Mengarini pursued his studies with the now restored Society of Jesus. Despite traditional Italian anti-clericalism, epitomized in the phrase, *"Siamo sotto le unghi dei preti"* [16] (we are under the talons of the priests), the young scholastic recognized in the Society, with its discipline and its program of service, a means of protesting, and perhaps altering existing social inequities. The emphasis placed by the Roman Catholic Church upon the corporal works of mercy, the value of deed in combination with a statement of faith offered a valid avenue for social renewal. It was an outlet ideally suited to Mengarini who during his life demonstrated that his penchant for ideals was felicitously combined with an unerring pursuit of the practical.

All of these or none of these factors may have contributed to the bouyant optimism evident in Mengarini's early correspondence from the North American missions. In an initial letter to Roothaan he praised the

---

15 William H. Stillman, *The Union of Italy* (Cambridge, Eng., 1909), p. 12.
16 Rolle, *Immigrant Upraised*, p. 24.

warm reception at Georgetown, saying "We find our-
selves joyful in each occupation and happy as we have
never been before." [17]

On April 24, 1841, Gregory Mengarini bid a permanent farewell to most ancient citadels of Christen-
dom. On that day he set out from St. Louis under the
captaincy of a grizzled trapper to breach a near-
impenetrable wilderness. In this enterprise he and his
cohorts would be joined by the first emigrant wagon
train to head overland for California. His leader, De
Smet, the inspiring young Fleming who had briefly
visited the Flatheads the year before noted: "Rev. Mr.
Mengarini recently from Rome, [was] specially selected by the Father General himself, for this mission
because of his age, his virtues, his great facility for
languages and his knowledge of medicine and music." [18]

The priest's abilities were well-summarized in one
description: "Mengarini was a man of tried virtue and
gentle nature, a skillful physician, a musician of no
mean order and a remarkable linguist." [19] He was
skilled in folk medicine and herbalism, and at the same
time pursued a native interest in the lore and mores of
the Indians. The product of this research was to appear
in American publications for the next half century.

Mengarini's virtues, however, equaled his accom-
plishments. His infrequent correspondence reveals a
generous temperament.[20] In describing a battle between
Blackfoot and Flatheads he noted: "The children who

17 Mengarini to Roothaan, Georgetown, Sept. 21, 1840, Mt. Sax., Vol. 1,
Fol. II, p. 2, GASJ.

18 Thwaites, *Early Western Travels*, XXVII, p. 193.

19 Rolle, *Immigrant Upraised*, p. 187, quoting from R. P. Laveille's *Le P.
De Smet, 1801-1873* (Liege, 1913).

20 Mengarini to Roothaan, Columbia River, Oct. 17, 1844, Mt. Sax., Vol. 11,
Fol. VII, p. 9, GASJ.

until then had demonstrated nothing but unconcern changed their indifference to tears which tore my heart, and then I did not see them but as poor little orphans exposed to all the fury of the enemies, most cruel against children as against armed men." [21]

Together with tenderness, Mengarini displayed an optimism to be envied. Before leaving St. Louis, he wrote to Father General at the behest of De Smet. With discerning candor he observed: "I do not know what trials the Lord has prepared for me. It is certain on many occasions I will be lacking, although a little common sense will help." He concluded the letter, however, with a statement of faith adding: ". . . I have a firm belief that God has called me and sent me to the ministry of his apostles so he will grant me to the last breath. . ." [22]

Explicitly expressed within the statement is an act of faith, an expression of evangelical zeal which was the *raison d'etre* for these lone expatriots. As Father Joseph Joset remarked: "Courage and patience are necessary to overcome the difficulties and bear the hardships inherent to their (mission) function." [23]

His annual reports to the Society in Rome are the best indicators of Mengarini's triumph over adversity and of his joyful satisfaction with the fractional steps toward change taken by his charges year by year. For example, it is with rightful enthusiasm that he reports that one-third of the Flatheads had mastered enough doctrine to qualify for Baptism on December 1, 1841.

---

[21] Mengarini to Roothaan, St. Mary's, June 30, 1848, Mt. Sax., Vol. 1, Fol. VII, p. 4, GASJ.

[22] Mengarini to Roothaan, St. Louis, Apr. 24, 1841, Mt. Sax., Vol. 1, Fol. II, p. 7, GASJ.

[23] Joseph Joset Papers, Box LXXXVIII, Jesuit Archives, Gonzaga Univ.

On another occasion he reports that prompted by fear that contact with Plains tribes might undo this initial religious transformation, Mengarini determined to ride with the Flatheads on their annual buffalo hunt in the spring of 1846. It is this zealous missionary ardor which underscores the gravity of the loss of his pack while fording a stream. He had undertaken the grueling over-land hunt in order to say Mass and administer the sacraments to his neophytes. Therefore, his disappoint-ment is real when he writes: "Imagine my feelings when I found that the articles thus lost were my blankets and provisions, and all the necessaries for saying Mass." The forlorn observation is followed by a rhetorical question and another profession of faith: "Should I go forward or go back. No blankets, no provisions, no Mass! Was it not the manifestation of God's will. . . But after all was not the accident rather the effect of carelessness than anything else?" He settled these doubts by "resolving to go ahead," and so he did.[24]

It should not be concluded that Mengarini the ad-ministrator and careful scholar had a tendency to romanticize and sentimentalize. Instead a single-minded commitment to the conversion of the Flatheads led him to assumptions about them and their motives which in light of subsequent developments, were ideal-ized. In describing the ceremony of the Feast of Pentecost he observed: "All [Flatheads] kept a pro-found silence but still the radiance of joy on their faces revealed the richness in their hearts – the ardor of the love in their innocent souls." [25]

---

[24] Mengarini, "Rocky Mountains," p. 144.

[25] Mengarini to Roothaan, St. Mary's, Nov. 14, 1843, Mt. Sax., Vol. 1, Fol. II, p. 8, GASJ. The "Memorie" abounds with such references.

Mengarini was neither a romantic nor a mystic, but rather a man compelled by a vision. In the largely untenanted wilderness where he struggled toward his missionary goal, adversity ground away what ever youthful flaws remained. He emerges in his letters and memoirs as patient and temperate, and above all humane and blessed by a saving wit. He was faithful to an Italian tradition, displaying a talent for turning a humorous phrase on every page of his reports to the august Father General with metaphors that never betray tedium or travail. Only Mengarini could capture the humor of the situation when in desperation he was forced to assign specific days for confession and communion to discourage requests for hourly confession from the newly baptized faithful. On another occasion, his insistence upon accompanying the buffalo hunters despite a sprained ankle is lightly explained: "They insisted I return to the village but as I did not consider that the accident warranted a non-compliance with an order of obedience, I insisted on going ahead." [26]

In describing the decrepit condition of St. Ignatius mission, which he claimed was as poor as St. Mary's, the beleaguered priest added that he was not sure whether the dogs or the pigs would be the ultimate victors in undermining the foundations. In either case, he allowed, the foundations' days were numbered. [27]

With regard to the inferior blue cloth used to replace the priest's cassocks, he ruefully observed: "If only Father General could see us now!" He explained that

---

[26] Mengarini here refers to one of the four vows taken by professed members of the Society. Partoll, "Mengarini's Narrative," p. 258.

[27] Mengarini to Roothaan, St. Mary's, Sept. 30, 1847, Mt. Sax., Vol. I, Fol. II, p. 2, GASJ.

it would take two years for the black wool ordered to replace their tattered soutanes to arrive. "Until the twenty pieces arrive from London in 1849, the priests must use the blue fabric the Hudson's Bay Company sells to the Indians to make leg coverings." [28]

It was with philosophic humor that he described the discovery that a party of visiting tribesmen, intently watching the Mass, had rested upon and bent the pipes of the organ he had struggled to have transported over the Rockies. His black curly head bent over the soundless keys as he lamented to De Smet: "There will be no music for Mass. We are indeed poor amidst great riches." [29]

Along with the saving wit which carried Mengarini through snow, cold and bitterroot broth, there was an abiding humility. The Flatheads' phenomenal devotion to the sacrament of penance he attributed to the catechetical zeal of the Flathead, Ambrose Scilcalemla, rather than to himself. He never hesitated to share the glory of his successful labor. Of one of his fellow missioners he wrote:

> Reverend Father De Vos remained at St. Mary's; he has wrought much good here, especially with the natives and the Canadians. I have never seen another man apply himself so diligently in learning another language as Father De Vos . . . he has stolen my dictionary and God knows when he will return it.[30]

Brother Claessens, the capable assistant, he observed, "is indefatigable. He does not save himself and does the work for many." Mengarini continued, revealing his

---

28 *Ibid.,* p. 3.

29 Patricia Corley, *Story of St. Mary's Mission,* p. 17; see also Mengarini, "Rocky Mountains," p. 34.

30 Mengarini to Roothaan, Vancouver, Sept. 26, 1844, [illegible citation], GASJ.

personal concern for each of his assistants: "But it seems that with time he is losing the use of his legs." [31]

Despite differences over allocations of budgets, Mengarini continued his warm admiration of Father Michael Accolti. At one point he pleaded with Vice Provincial Peter Beckx that Accolti not be removed from the Oregon missions explaining:

> God gave him a particular quality difficult to find in others of winning in a few moments of conversation the hearts of his listeners, especially Americans who knew nothing about Catholicism . . . Father Accolti had become a public figure beginning from the governor of Oregon (all Protestant) even to the workmen. It was only necessary that he would preach and the Church would be filled with Protestants.[32]

Nor did Mengarini spare himself from manual labor and menial tasks. He was among the first to raise the timbers for the mission church. In an effort to involve the men of the tribe and to make the church a joint accomplishment, the new pastor, ". . . began to preach from Genesis, 'You will earn your bread by the sweat of your brow.'" To his satisfaction he added, "They began then, at least the chiefs, to put their hands to work." [33]

An unrelenting diligence emerges as Mengarini casually describes a serious illness he suffered while the tribe was hunting in mid-December 1842. So weakened that he could no longer retain food, perpetually as cold as ice, and finally emaciated beyond recognition, the lonely Jesuit continued to celebrate Mass, give two

---

[31] Mengarini to Roothaan, St. Mary's, Sept. 30, 1847, Mt. Sax., Vol. 1, Fol. I, p. 33, GASJ.

[32] Mengarini to Vice Provincial Peter Beckx, Champoeg, Jan. 15, 1855, Mt. Sax., Vol. 2, Fol. I, p. 11, GASJ.

[33] Mengarini to Roothaan, Vancouver, Sept. 26, 1844, [illegible citation], GASJ.

daily instructions, and on Saturdays hear one hundred confessions.

As the shadows of evening climbed the walls of his cabin, the Reverend Mengarini would huddle by the hearth making ornaments for the church. In spite of his weakness, he used his resourceful imagination to create an atmosphere of ecclesiastical ceremony to inspire the Indians. Offhandedly, he described his clever handicraft:

> With two pieces of white muslin and two red handkerchiefs I made a throne; with two gold leaves I covered a *raggera* of wood; and with some brass ornaments I made a monstrance which was fairly decent, candlebra and cornacopia in quantity as well, so that on Easter Sunday I could present a miniature spectacle of what had been presented at the Roman College during Forty Hours Devotion.[34]

In the winter stillness, or when the village was empty during buffalo hunting season, the Italian priest perhaps felt a faint shiver of strangeness, and, no doubt, yearned backward to his boyhood days near the Tiber. But the loneliness of command among an unfamiliar people and an anxiety which always lurked at the edge of his awareness were all surmounted by his curiosity and enterprise. Far into the night, for example, Mengarini labored to learn yet another language. Master of flawless Italian and Latin, a fluent writer and conversationalist in Spanish and French, he now added the Salish language. Witnesses reported with surprise that when Mengarini spoke in his newly adopted tongue, none knew whether it was a Flathead or a European who spoke. Soon the frontier philologist composed a

---

[34] *Ibid.*

basic grammar of the Salishan tongue, still unsurpassed as the standard reference for the cognate dialects.

It was by firelight, after his day among the faithful Flathead, that Mengarini began to work on the Salish dictionary. Only when the disheartened missioner left the territory for California did he bequeath his manuscript to the young Jesuits who would eventually publish it on the press originally transported westward by Protestant missioners.[35]

Having mastered this new tongue, Mengarini was eager to learn more about his comrades, adding:

> As my knowledge of Flathead increased, I was naturally curious to learn from our Indians the history, traditions and mythology of their tribe. I therefore gathered together some of the most respected among them and questioned them upon these matters: One answered my questions, and the others nodded their approval of his answers. *Of their past history they knew nothing.* Nor is this to be wondered at, since the Indian is a being of the present day, caring nothing for what is past, and leaving the future to take care of itself, provided that he has plenty to eat today.[36]

This disposition toward linguistic and ethnographic research also led Mengarini to study the Indians of Oregon, and in later years, to compile a vocabulary of the Santa Clara Indians.[37] Father Mengarini's additional contribution to philology is his *Selish or Flathead Grammar,* published in 1861 from the third manuscript copy, the first two laboriously handwritten

---

[35] Thwaites, *Early Western Travels,* XXVII, p. 193, note 69.

[36] Mengarini, "Rocky Mountains," p. 34. (Italics supplied.) The result of this research represents a significant portion of the "Memorie."

[37] See "Preface," note 8, herein, for a bibliographic summary of Mengarini's works.

copies having been lost through carelessness or accident. He also initiated work on the vocabulary of the cognate Salishan languages, later published by his successors in the Rocky Mountain missions.

Hours devoted to work and study were also filled with the expanding joy of accomplishment, and a fortitude which was impatient with the loneliness which sometimes marbled Mengarini's days. Life in the pathless wild, beyond the edge of the frontier, where letters from family and even the Society arrived with good fortune every two years, demanded an inner resourcefulness to survive in solitude the inexorable passage of time. Mengarini used the virtues to advantage. His membership in the delegation to the Blackfeet, avowed enemies of the Flathead, and in his estimation, ruthless warriors of the Plains, demonstrated that isolation amidst the "Great Stonies" had not robbed him of his cool, easy courage. The Little Faro uprising of 1847 again underscored Mengarini's self-assurance, his self-discipline and his ultimate leadership of the tribe. Only his quick, sure judgment temporarily forestalled the bleak end of the "mission in the mountains."

Mengarini was equally self-assured when coping with the interminable bureaucracy of the Hudson's Bay Company, or even that of the Society itself. He minced no words in bringing to the attention of the Father General the inequitable distribution of funds and supplies among the missions in the Oregon Country. He presented a painfully clear case illustrating the inefficiency of the Society's procurement system, supported by facts and figures proving the exorbitance of the

Hudson's Bay Company prices as well as the indulgent extravagance of certain members of the Society.[38]

In his yearly report to Father General Roothaan dated September 30, 1847, Mengarini clearly and pointedly outlined the defects in the Society's system of order and supply. First, he noted that the original church and home, made to serve for three weeks, was still in use after six years though twenty-two supports were needed to keep it standing. "We have been at various times forced to escape quickly in order to avoid the rats. When it rains, if the snow deepens, we cannot say Mass."[39]

He hastened to add that if the Order would not deposit the mission funds with the Hudson's Bay Company via the English Jesuit Procurator, Father George Jenkins in London, but instead send it directly to the missions, he could buy at one-third the price from the competing American Fur Company. Here again Mengarini proposed a practical solution. Armed with a volume of facts and figures he observed that little more than "15,000 francs in all have been received by the three missions in the mountains" in the past three years. Driving home his point, he concluded, "This subtracted from the 190,000 francs allocated to the missions during the period, leaves about 175,000." He left the question of the disappearing balance to be answered by the astute Father General.[40]

Nor did the difficulties end there. He added that

---

[38] Mengarini to Roothaan, Vancouver, Sept. 26, 1844, [illegible citation], GASJ.

[39] Mengarini to Roothaan, St. Mary's, Sept. 30, 1847, Mt. Sax., Vol. I, Fol. II, p. 33, GASJ.   [40] *Ibid.*

what was ordered two years before was seldom what arrived two years later after passage through the many bureaucratic channels. "At the same time," he added, "the missions close to the forts at Walla Walla and Colville easily avail themselves of these sources for flour, animals, and all else they need, including the repair of their plows, etc." [41]

Perhaps because of these impolitic assertions, or perhaps because of his unflinching insistence that the existing missions be properly staffed before any plans for expansion be considered, his profession was delayed. Finally, on December 9, 1850, Gregory Mengarini was admitted to the professed of the Society, taking the fourth vow of loyalty to the papacy, a rare and high honor for any Jesuit.

No doubt, Father Accolti's earlier letter to Father General Roothaan which contained an unrestrained appraisal of the young Roman's work contributed to his advance.

> Father Mengarini is the only outstanding missionary who does what is expected of him and in reality receives very little help, and if abandoning the Indians would not result in an uprising, I would advance the proposition that he be professed. . . While on this subject, Your Paternity, allow me to express my surprise that this forgotten missionary has not yet been advanced to profession in light of his zeal, his singular abilities with the Flathead language, as well as other talents which should be considered along with his seniority. Instead, *Mengarini exemplifies the qualities the Society associates with the rank of professed.*[42]

Even after the heartbreaking termination to his

---

41 *Ibid.*

42 Father Michael Accolti to Roothaan, Santa Clara, Calif., Feb. 29, 1850, Mt. Sax., GASJ. (Italics supplied.)

labors at St. Mary's mission, Mengarini, the administrator, proved to be the salvation of the Oregon Mission.
In 1853 he wrote to Rev. Francis Pellico in Rome:
"I must have the wherewithal to buy provisions for the
coming year, otherwise I will pay six per cent interest
and we will again be dependent upon the Hudson's Bay
Company." [43] Apparently, the plea was effective, for
next year's report included a thanks for the sum "sufficient to pay all three years' debts." [44]

Even when fairly well-established and involved in
the affairs of Santa Clara College in California, Mengarini did not hesitate to briskly assess a plan to unite
several of the Rocky Mountain tribes into one mission.
In clear and precise language he determined that the
proposal was "in fact impossible." Nor did he want for
reasons, adding that "it takes more than a few days to
understand the state of the missions." [45]

As the years passed, his administrative and teaching
skills contributed to both the success and solvency of
Santa Clara, and although he longed for the tribal
lands, he resisted the entreaties of the Flathead delegation led by Chief Victor. Amidst the varied enterprises
of this new life, time crept by unnoticed, and time
turned years into decades. Finally, in 1881 a stroke
partially paralyzed Mengarini. Soon failing eyesight
forced him to discontinue the reading of the Divine
Office and the celebration of the Mass.

On September 23, 1886, Mengarini rose as usual, and

---

[43] Mengarini to Father [Francis] Pellico, Oregon City, Nov. 1853, Mt. Sax.,
Vol. 2, Fol. I, p. 4, GASJ.

[44] Mengarini to Beckx, Champoeg, Jan. 15, 1855, [illegible citation], GASJ.

[45] Mengarini to Beckx, Santa Clara, Dec. 11, 1855, Mt. Sax., Vol. 2, Fol. II,
p. 13, GASJ.

pursued his pleasant ritual, visiting the garden and the vineyard. At noon, however, he was not at his place in the refectory; instead he lay on the floor of his room. Though his pulse still beat, a third stroke had done its work.[46]

The Last Rites of the Church were administered to this man of two worlds who had crossed the Atlantic to join the vanguard of missioners into the Rockies to teach, to preach, to practice the works of mercy. This patrician pioneer unwittingly marked the epochs of frontier expansion as a witness to the first emigrant wagon train to California, as the first white resident among the Flatheads, and as co-developer of the first college in California. For none of these has he been honored, but he must be reckoned among the scholars of the American West for yet another labor. What appears as *inter alia* in the career of a missionary educator distinguishes him as an ethnohistorian of merit. His "Memorie," valuable remnant of his life among the Flatheads, provides a record unsurpassed by later chroniclers. Mengarini's recollections mirror the life he and his band lived safely beyond the Hell Gate defile. He wrote of the Indians' past and of the new arcadia he so ardently wished to provide for them from the day he first heard their plea which echoed across the continents and inspired his missionary vision.

---

46 "A Career Ended," San Francisco *Morning Call*, Sept. 25, 1886, p.b., col. 2; *Vita Functi in Societati Iesu*, 7 Aug. 1814- 7 Aug. 1914 (Paris 1897), p. 7; *Vita Functi Provincial Oregiensis* (Portland, Oreg., 1960), p. 17.

A New Arcadia

In the region extending from the Yellowstone National Park along what is the now the boundary line between Montana and Idaho is a range of mountains broadly sweeping from west to north from the United States into Canada. Beyond the 46° latitude to the Cordillerean upsurge it is not known as the Rockies but as the Bitterroot Range. In the long and narrow plain shadowed by its ragged peaks, the long-sought Black Robes settled with the devoted Flatheads. These tribal lands lying in the extreme western portion of Montana between the Continental Divide on the east and the Bitterroot Range on the west had been their habitat since at least the beginning of the seventeenth century. Some culture patterns of the Flatheads "suggest that possibly they were more recent arrivals from Asia than most native Americans." These Indians who called themselves "the Salish, variously rendered as Selish, Salees, Selic, Silix, Selictcen, etc." may have traveled south along the western borders of the Plains, through the Rocky Mountain Trench or through western British Columbia.[1]

---

[1] Olga W. Johnson, *Flathead and Kootenay,* pp. 40-41. The study provides extensive information regarding the background and life ways of both tribes.

During a portion of each year they paused in the valley long enough to harvest the bitterroot and camas. In this basin drained by the Clark's Fork of the Columbia, between the present town of Stevensville and the ruins of old Fort Owen, St. Mary's mission was established.[2] Since it was already September when the company of missionaries arrived, it was important to choose a site for a reduction where at least temporary shelters could be erected.[3] The valley was protected from the Blackfoot on the south by a chain of mountains, was sheltered from the north by timbered slopes. Through it ran the river the Flatheads called the Bitterroot.

Since most of the significant events of the long trip had occurred on some feast of the Blessed Virgin, the mission was to be called St. Mary's.[4] Father Nicolas Point was immediately commissioned to apply his artistic talent in drawing up a plan for a residence for the missionaries, a church and utility building.[5] Finally, the mission to the Flatheads was to be a reality.

The Fathers were no less impressed with these ardent suppliants for the faith than earlier visitors had been. Though the leader of the welcoming delegation, Oulstilpo, had claimed: "I am only an evil and ignorant man." De Smet reserved his highest praise for the tribe:

[2] "Montana's First White Settlement at Stevensville by Missionaries in 1841," *Stevensville* (Mont.) *Register,* Dec. 23, 1909, p. 1, col. 2.

[3] Reductions were systems of Indian settlement successfully developed by the Jesuits in Paraguay where the converted Indians were, while learning crafts and trades as well as the rubrics of their new religion, kept strictly apart from the white settlers.

[4] Point includes in his narrative the account of the vision of the Blessed Virgin Mary beheld by a young girl at the exact future site of the mission. Point, *Wilderness Kingdom,* p. 42.

[5] This may be the town plan Mengarini refers to at the conclusion of the "Memorie." Most likely, it was similar to that which Point drew for the Coeur d'Alene Mission.

The Flatheads are disinterested, generous, devoted to their brethren and friends; irreproachable, and even exemplary, as regards probity and morality. Among them, dissensions, quarrels, injuries and enmities are unknown.[6]

There is unequivocal agreement in historical annals regarding the fact that the Flatheads were considered superior Indians by allies, enemies and visitors alike. Traders, uniformly impressed by their character and integrity as compared with other tribes, extravagantly extolled their friendliness, honesty, frankness, and praised their truthfulness, courage, cleanliness, obedience to their chiefs and the chastity of their women.[7] In fact, admiration was often unabashed. All traders had favorite tribes, but "almost without exception" the frontiersmen spoke with respect and sometimes even with fondness of the Nez Perce and particularly, the Flatheads. "All that was good about Indian society seemed embodied in these tribes," wrote Peter Skene Ogden. A man known for his devastating realism and candor, Ogden did not hesitate to choose "the Flatheads as his favorites."[8]

Not only were the Flatheads admired, but they were actively defended from detractors as well. When a captivity narrative of dubious authenticity described bondage, torture, and indignities at the hands of the Flatheads, William H. Ashley wrote an indignant letter to the editor of a St. Louis newspaper, operating on "a desire to do justice to those who have it not in their power to vindicate themselves." The fur-trade pioneer challenged the integrity of the author and proceeded

---

[6] Thwaites, *Early Western Travels*, xxv, p. 287.

[7] Jack Fahey, *The Flatheads*. The volume provides an authoritative summary of Flathead history and tradition.

[8] Lewis O. Saum, *The Fur Trader and the Indian*, p. 57.

to offer a generous and heartwarming character reference for the Flatheads.[9]

A description of the Flatheads by Major Peter Ronan, penned shortly after Father Mengarini launched St. Mary's mission, notes that both sexes were slender and fair, "their complexions a shade lighter than the palest new copper after being freshly rubbed." Both men and women wore garments of dressed deer skin ornamented with fringes to which the women added beads, hawk bills and thimbles. Their clothes were regularly cleaned with the pipe clay which abounds in the area.[10] One of the most talented to portray the tribe observed: ". . . it must be admitted that in the eyes of the vain man the costume of an Indian riding through camp at a full gallop is not without its charm."[11]

After the closing of the mission in 1850, Lieutenant John Mullan expressed similar admiration for the Flatheads. Equal esteem was expressed in a report made by Territorial Governor Isaac Stevens to President Franklin Pierce who included the glowing accolade in his annual message to Congress: "They [the Flatheads] are the best Indians of the Territory, honest, brave and docile."[12]

As for the physical disfiguration which the name Flathead implies, there is no evidence in historic time to justify it. Even though the French voyageurs called

[9] *Ibid.*

[10] Maj. Peter Ronan, *Historical Sketch of the Flathead Indian Nation from the Year 1813 to 1890,* p. 9.

[11] Fortunately an enviable gallery of Flathead portraits and genre studies were painted by Nicolas Point, S.J. In the 1850s Gustavus Sohon, an interpreter for Lt. John Mullan while exploring the Bitterroot Valley, made nine pencil portraits of prominent Flathead leaders. These latter were presented to the U.S. National Museum in 1883. John C. Ewers, *Gustavus Sohon,* p. 12.

[12] Robert Ignatius Burns, *The Jesuit and the Indian Wars of the Northwest,* p. 8.

them the *Tetes plattes* the Flatheads denied the practice of head flattening, saying "How could we have done this . . . when our cradleboards before the mothers had horses to ride were too short for binding babies heads to?"[13] Neighboring tribes traditionally believe, however, that when the Flatheads first arrived from the lower Columbia, they practiced the head shaping or deforming typical among the latter tribes. The explanation offered by contemporary Flatheads is that in sign language the symbol for the tribe is often interpreted as "pressed side of head" or "pressed head," hence Flathead.

Although insulated by mountain barriers, the Flatheads shared in the transmission of Plains culture traits. For example, Spanish horses transmitted by Apache raiders to Shoshone traders reached the interior basin by 1725 at the latest.[14] This resulting mobility extended the perimeter of Flathead contact as well as contributed to more efficient acquisition of food. Consequently, Plains culture traits associated with the war complex, along with the tipi, buck-skin clothing and rituals like the scalp dance were assimilated by the Salish-speaking tribes of the Interior Columbia Plateau.

Only in time of war did the Salish adopt the tribal organization patterns to the south. They instead maintained a loose organization of village life which lent itself to patterns of seasonal migration more closely resembling an agglomeration of villages than a tribe.[15]

---

[13] Johnson, *Flathead and Kootenay*, p. 164.

[14] Evidence of Flathead participation in the horse complex is found in the journals of Lewis and Clark. "The Indians were mounted on very fine horses of which the Flatheads had a great abundance; that is, each man in the nation possesses from twenty to a hundred head." Bernard DeVoto, ed., *Journals of Lewis and Clark* (Boston, 1953), p. 236.

[15] Burns, *The Jesuit and Indian Wars*, pp. 10-11.

The regular migrations in search of food presented one of the greatest obstacles to the Jesuits. In spring and summer the Flathead resided in the Bitterroot Valley, living on camas roots, berries and small game. In June and July the men crossed the mountains for a brief hunt to obtain meat and hides. Again, after the end of the berry season in September and October, the entire tribe would move to the plains near the upper tributaries of the Missouri River, returning to dig bitterroot in March or April. Thus the Flatheads were involved in a long winter hunt for fully half a year.

Although the neighboring Kutenai, Pend d'Oreille and Shoshone recognized the territorial rights of the Flathead on the plains during the migratory buffalo hunts, the Blackfeet pushing southwestward from Alberta toward the Rockies and the northern tributaries of the northern Missouri presented a formidable challenge. Armed with guns and a ready supply of shot and powder obtained from white traders along the Saskatchewan and also mounted on swift horses, they ruthlessly attacked the Shoshones, Flatheads and Kutenais, still armed only with primitive bows, arrows and lances. Consequently, by the end of the eighteenth century the Blackfeet had become masters of the northwestern plains. Years later a middle-aged Flathead recalled, "the hectic days of his youth when his courageous people . . . decided to leave the plains to find peace behind the Rocky Mountain barrier." [16]

16 John C. Ewers, *The Blackfeet, Raiders on the Northwestern Plains,* pp. 30-52. Also consult Lewis H. Morgan, "Indian Migrations," *The Indian Miscellany,* ed. by William W. Beach; Oscar Lewis, "The Effects of White Contact Upon Blackfoot Culture with Special Reference to the Role of the Fur Trade," *Monographs of the Am. Ethn. Soc.,* VI, pp. 1-73.

In the face of this threat, western tribes banded together to form large scale hunting expeditions on the
plains. They also began to seek new tools and rituals
to protect them. By the first decade of the nineteenth
century, Crow Indians who had secured guns from the
Mandans and Hidatsa began trading them with the
Shoshones and Flatheads.[17] By 1808 and 1809 the Flatheads also secured guns from Canadian traders after
David Thompson and Finan McDonald had built
North West Fur Company trading posts near them. By
1810 the Flatheads, armed with twenty guns supplied
by traders, had successfully subdued their enemies,
killing sixteen Piegans who had dared refer to the Shoshones and by implication, their allies, the Flatheads,
as "miserable old women whom they could kill with
sticks and stones."[18]

The Flatheads were now in a position to retaliate
against Blackfoot harassment and horse theft and to
enforce their prior right to hunt the buffalo on the
plains. Despite an offer made by Ross Cox to negotiate
a peace between the warring factions, the bloody conflict continued through the mid-nineteenth century,
ultimately contributing to the closing of Mengarini's
mission at St. Mary's in 1850.

While the Blackfeet waged intermittent war, the
Flathead cultivated friendly relations with both American and British fur traders. In return for peltries, the

[17] The Crows also served as middlemen in transmitting articles of European manufacture, such as brass kettles, which the western tribesmen cut into
small pieces to ornament their hair and clothing. François Laroque, *Journal
of Laroque from the Assiniboine to the Yellowstone 1805* (Ottawa, 1905), pp.
71-72.

[18] Ewers, *The Blackfeet*, p. 30.

Salish acquired practical objects as well as luxuries, blue cloth, and beads which were as desirable as utensils, tools and gunpowder. It was as a result of this fur trade activity that a group of Iroquois probably trained at the Jesuit mission of Caughnawaga, settled and inter-married with them in the first half of the century.

As Mengarini explains in the "Memorie," the Iro-quois, particularly Ignace La Mouse, introduced cer-tain elements of Catholic worship into the primitive ceremonials which Captain Benjamin L. E. Bonneville noted in the early 1830s.[19] They observed, as well, the cardinal holidays of the Roman Catholic Church. Sun-day was considered a day of rest devoted to religious instruction interspersed with singing and dancing. The remainder of the day the Flatheads indulged their love of gambling, enthusiastically wagering on horse races and playing the "hand game."

It was these Iroquois who had encouraged the organ-ization of a series of deputations to St. Louis in the 1830s in search of a "Black Robe." It was in answer to this request that De Smet and his band of Jesuit priests and lay brothers set out from Westport, Missouri, in 1841 to attempt to establish in the uncharted Indian territory of the North American continent centers for religious and socio-economic training similar to those they had successfully developed in South America.

Unfortunately, the records and diaries of early St. Mary's have never been located. Quite possibly they were lost after the closing of the mission in 1850, for Father Ravalli writes that two-thirds of what was car-

19 Washington Irving, *The Adventures of Captain Bonneville, U.S.A.*, ed. by Edgely W. Todd (Norman, Okla., 1964), p. 116.

ried away from the mission was lost in the waters, presumably while fording rivers.[20] Consequently, the events following De Smet's encounter with Big Face, the principal chief of the Flathead tribe, must be drawn from unofficial accounts. From the Nicolas Point narrative, we learn of the illness of their official interpreter and the sudden destructive hurricane which threatened to demolish the temporary buildings on December 3, the day before the Feast of St. Francis Xavier when two hundred and two catechumens were to be baptized.[21]

Mengarini's "Narrative of the Rockies" offers an even more detailed litany of those initial trials. He begins with a description of the construction of the log cabin, a church and "a sort of fort protected by bastions." Since it was fall, the earth was already frozen and the trench for the foundation had to be cut with axes. The Indians seemed singularly disinclined to fell the trees in the forest nearby and haul them to the building site, he observed. Thus in frustration Mengarini decided, "Example is better than precept," and seizing an axe he began to work. Some half-breeds attempted to deter him, advising that such behavior would cause him to lose authority. While they chided, Mengarini swung his axe. Soon a chief, "throwing down his buffalo robe," asked for an axe. The others followed and the construction progressed beyond expectation.[22]

In his reminiscences, the transplanted Roman adds

---

[20] Schoenberg, "Memorandum Regarding St. Mary's Existing Log Church," ms., Jes. Arch., Gonzaga Univ.

[21] Point, *Wilderness Kingdom,* p. 42.

[22] Partoll, "Mengarini's Narrative," p. 197.

with ironic humor that one should not sneer at this first building, although the cracks between the interlacing logs were filled with clay, and "the partitions between the rooms were of deer-skin." Furthermore, he adds that "the roof of saplings was covered with straw and earth. The windows were 2 x 1, and deer-skin with the hair scraped off supplied the place of glass." [23]

In a few weeks' time, the log chapel was completed. The primitive structure had no floor, no pews. Nevertheless, a Solemn Mass of dedication was offered in the new shrine on the first Sunday in October – The Feast of Our Lady of The Holy Rosary. Resplendent in gaily beaded costumes, the proud members of the congregation sat in semi-circles on the bare ground facing the altar. A fire smoldering on the dirt floor, with smoke escaping upward through a hole in the roof, dispelled the chill of the autumn morning which witnessed the formal opening of the Mission of St. Mary's in the Flathead country.

The progress made by the Flatheads under the direction of Fathers Point and Mengarini impressed De Smet upon his return from Fort Colville in late fall. He wrote to Father General Roothaan that the "plan" had been "carried into execution." [24]

The plan was similar to that developed by the Society in Paraguay. De Smet referred to his missions as "reductions," a term borrowed from the South American system in which nomadic neophytes were also taught to be farmers and artisans. According to De Smet, the field west of the Rocky Mountains presented many

23 Mengarini, "Rocky Mountains," pp. 306-07.

24 De Smet to Roothaan, St. Mary's, Dec. 30, 1841, cited in Chittenden and Richardson, De Smet, I, p. 330.

similarities to the condition of the native races of South America. In both the main obstacle to conversion had been the example and blatant vice of the whites. Consequently, De Smet scrupulously attempted to adhere to his *Vade Mecum* (a personal translation) of the narrative of Giovanni Muratori, the historian of the Paraguay missions.[25]

In essence the application of the principles of the reductions by the Society in the Oregon Territory was:

> Law, government, family, all is modeled upon and conforms to the principles of true Christian civilization and to the directions given to this new Reduction by the missionaries. Guiding and inspiring us are the impressive accomplishments of the famous missions of Paraguay, described in great detail in Muratori's, *Il Christianismo Felice*.[26]

De Smet described the system as consisting of four steps: (1) the nurturing of a simple, firm faith; (2) a respect for authority; (3) industry and a love of labor; (4) flight from all contaminating influences or from what the Gospel calls the world.[27]

Jesuit procedures in their Montana reductions more or less followed this pattern. A site for a mission was carefully selected and developed. The rudiments of a basically agricultural economy were imparted to the Indians, partly for the obvious purpose of civilizing them, and partly to bring them within the range of the missionaries for spiritual guidance. From this mission center, then, the Jesuits radiated outward, like spokes

---

[25] Giovanni Muratori, *Il Cristianismo Felice, in Missione Della Provincia Torinese Della Compagnia Di Gesu Nelle Montagne Rocciose Della America Settentrionale* (Turin, 1863).

[26] Giovanni Muratori, *Il Christiansimo Felice,* cited in *Missione Delle Provincia Torinese Della Compagnie di Gesu,* p. 5.

[27] Chittenden and Richardson, *De Smet,* I, pp. 328-29.

in a wheel, into numberless valleys and plateaus. In this way eight distinct centers were established and from these the Jesuits worked, covering most of the state well before the end of the nineteenth century.

The basis of the missionary operation was relatively simple. The Jesuits set out two by two "with little more than a staff and a prayerbook." Accompanied by several Indian neophytes as interpreters, they would address each new tribe stressing the inconveniences of Indians' present way of life – the problematic food supply, the discomfort of their dwellings and their "defenseless condition" in the frequent wars in which they were engaged. The priests then "invited them to come and live together in some settled spot, to build houses, and to cultivate the ground." [28]

Thus, when De Smet, having left October 28, returned on December 8, 1841, with provisions and farm implements purchased from the Hudson's Bay Company at Fort Colville three hundred miles away, he could report:

> The Flatheads, assisting us with their whole heart and strength, had, in a short time, cut from two to three thousand stakes; and the three brothers, with no other tools than the axe, saw and auger, constructed a chapel with pediment, colonnade and gallery, balustrade, choir, seats &c. by St. Martin's day; when they assembled in the little chapel all the catechumens, and continued the instructions which were to end on the third of December, the day fixed for their baptism.[29]

The Indians valued the chickens, hogs and cows De Smet had returned with, but the seeds he brought from Fort Colville, which consisted of a few bushels of oats,

---

28 Schoenberg, *Jesuits in Montana*, p. 6.
29 Thwaites, *Early Western Travels*, XXVII, p. 310.

wheat and potatoes, caused consternation among the Indians. As planting season arrived, they watched the sowing and planting with curiosity and criticism. They thought it very foolish for the Fathers to tear up the soil and grass for their ponies and then bury in the ground that which seemed good to eat. It was incredible to them that under the soil the seed would reproduce itself, despite the reassurances of Brother William Claessens. They would, therefore, spend hour after hour, day after day, perched on the fence awaiting the appearance of the first shoots marking the beginning of agriculture in Montana.[30]

"Thus did the material and the spiritual temple of the Divine Master progress among them," wrote Mengarini, while he disconsolately added that polygamy and the magic sumesch cult defiantly continued.[31] Nevertheless, De Smet was able to write by Christmas: "The Flathead nation had been converted – four hundred Kalispels baptized, eighty Nez Perce, several Coeurs d'Alene, many Kootenays, Blackfeet, Snakes and Bannacs."[32] Six to seven hundred new Christians crowded into the small chapel decorated with rushes to celebrate the Solemn Mass of Thanksgiving with Father De Smet. Faithful to their promise, the Indians had returned from the hunt before the beginning of winter. With them they brought seventy bales of dried meat for the Jesuits, nearly three tons to be eaten with grease and berries, or berries and grease!

---

[30] Palladino, *Indian and White in the Northwest*, pp. 37-38; William P. Donnelly, "Nineteenth Century Jesuit Reductions in the United States," *Mid-America*, XVII (Jan. 1935), p. 75; Helen C. Clark, "Black Robes Taught Farming," *Great Falls* (Mont.) *Tribune*, July 28, 1968, p. 23.

[31] Mengarini, "Rocky Mountains," p. 308.

[32] Thwaites, *Early Western Travels*, XXVII, p. 319.

On December 3, the feast of St. Francis Xavier, Father Mengarini, despite his indisposition, gathered the two hundred catechumens in the solemn candlelight of the log chapel, covered with mats of rushes and festoons of green on the walls and ceiling. The thirteen who were considered qualified to serve as sponsors, as well as the Great Chief Paul, a nonegenarian, who had been baptized two years before, witnessed the entire interrogation, which, "except for the time taken for dinner . . . lasted from six o'clock in the morning until nine o'clock at night." [33] Perhaps the eager acceptance of this new doctrine rests upon the fact that the miraculous and inexplicable, so much a part of Catholicism, adapted itself easily to the Flathead Somésch quest concept.[34]

An organized system of instruction patterned on that used by the Brothers of the Christian Doctrine in Rome was followed. Catholic doctrine was summarized in several hundred questions and answers to be committed to memory. During the daily hour of instruction, interspersed with song, tickets of approbation were given to those who answered correctly. The tickets served to indicate attendance, express approval, and since indicating a measure of mastery, prompted parents to urge improvement in the children. The device thus involved the entire community.

The method of instruction was to reduce the Catechism to question and answer forms. These were committed to memory and on appointed dates "cat-

[33] Point, *Wilderness Kingdom,* p. 42.
[34] Alan P. Merriam, *Ethnomusicology of the Flathead Indians* (Chicago, 1967).

echism bees" were held in church. Contestants asked questions of each other until disqualified by failure to answer correctly. The contests were limited to children "for in the children lay the future greatness of the missions." [35]

Another favored device employed with success by the missionaries was to assign one phrase of a prayer to each group of children. Then placing each child in the proper position, the whole of the prayer was recited, phrase by phrase, until they knew the prayer as a unit.[36]

Father Mengarini and Father Point may also have utilized the "Catholic Ladder" or the "Sah-kah-lee Stick," purportedly developed by Father Francis Blanchet during his evangelization of the Indians of the Pacific Northwest. On the long stick were cut forty short parallel lines or notches giving the appearance of a ladder. Each line or notch represented a century, and the whole forty represented the traditional four thousand years of the world's history prior to the advent of Christ. These lines were followed by thirty-three points or dots and three crosses to show the years of Christ's life and the manner of his death. A church and twelve perpendicular marks denoted the beginnings of the Church at the death of Christ, through the twelve apostles. Eighteen further horizontal lines or marks (each a century) and thirty-nine points (each a year) indicated the lapse of time since the death of Christ.[37]

[35] Bischoff, *Jesuits in Old Oregon,* p. 31.

[36] Donnelly, "Jesuit Reductions," p. 76.

[37] Charles M. Buchanan, "The Catholic Ladder," *The Indian Sentinel,* VII (Jan. 1918), p. 22. Point portrays this device in a sketch reproduced in *Wilderness Kingdom,* p. 85. Another device developed by Father Francis Blanchet in 1839 was a carved wooden timeline called the "Jesus Stick."

Of course, the religious life of the community also included the adults. Mengarini hastened to add:

> When the Angelus rings, the Indians rise from sleep; half an hour after the morning prayers are said in common; all assist at Mass and at the instruction. A second instruction is given in evening at sunset and lasts about an hour and a quarter . . . One of the Fathers each morning visits the sick, to furnish them with medicines, and give them such assistance as their wants may require.[38]

Father Point wrote upon returning from the winter hunt, to what was now an enclosed farm and village, that he joined the other priests in preparing the Indians for the reception of the sacraments of Penance and Holy Communion in order that they make their Easter duty. Point goes on to say: "Pentecost Sunday of 1842 was the most beautiful day that had ever shone on the village of St. Mary's for on this day its elite received for the first time the Bread of Angels."[39]

In summarizing the effect on the first year's missionary activities, De Smet observed that in addition to the baptisms at which he officiated in the spring of 1842, and "with 500 baptized last year, in different parts of the country, mostly among the Flatheads and Kalispels, and 196 that I baptized on Christmas day, at St. Mary's, with the 350 baptized by Rev. Fathers Mengarini and Point, make a total of 1654 souls, wrested from the power of the devil."[40]

"At the first tolling of the bell, they ran with great speed to the church," Mengarini observed, "as a band

---

[38] Chittenden and Richardson, *De Smet,* I, p. 336.

[39] Point, *Wilderness Kingdom,* p. 46.

[40] Thwaites, *Early Western Travels,* XXVII, pp. 381-82.

of famished to an oven of baking bread." [41] The religious fervor of the Flathead is also frequently attested to by Father De Smet, who wrote: "The Flatheads are fond of praying. After the regular evening prayer, they will assemble in their tents to pray or sing canticles. These pious exercises will frequently be prolonged till a late hour; and if any wake during the night, they begin to pray." On Sundays, the exercises of devotion were longer and more numerous, the Indians seemingly unfatigued by their pious ceremonials. According to De Smet, they felt that the happiness of the little and the humble was to speak with their Heavenly Father, and "no house presented so many attractions as did the house of the Lord." [42]

In contrast, the chronicle of the Flatheads' musical education is somewhat less impressive, but no less a tribute to Mengarini's ardor, and his sense of humor. Soon after arriving he had translated several canticles into the Flathead tongue. The music for two he had composed himself. As time passed, the young priest also organized a band which he described as a "conglomerate affair," consisting of a flute, two accordions, a tambourine, a piccolo, cymbals and a bass drum. The young musicians quickly learned to read the notes, for their teacher proudly wrote: "Indians have excellent

[41] Mengarini to Roothaan, Mar. 10, 1842, ms., Jes. Arch., Gonzaga Univ.

[42] This possible tendency on the part of the missionaries to idealize the behavior of their Indian disciples is revealed in an episode Father De Smet related much later to Thurlow Weed. He then admitted that he and his Indians had discovered gold in the Black Hills, but not until years after did his Indian friends admit that the gold they had discovered had been found on a man they had murdered. "Letter from John Maguire," *Daily Territorial Enterprise* (Virginia City, Nev.), June 22, 1875, quoted in *Cont. to the Hist. Soc. of Mont.,* VIII (1917), p. 152.

eyes and ears for music." If the group was weak in numbers, he added, it was most certainly "strong in lungs." Those playing "wind instruments spared neither contortions of the face nor exertions of their organs to give volume to their music." [43]

As a result of their enthusiasm for non-Indian music, Mengarini began teaching music to several youngsters and the ablest of the catechumens in 1843. From this group, he formed a military band consisting of two clarinets, two accordions, three ottoviani and three flutes. By Easter the group was ready to perform in Church. In the annual report to the Father General, Mengarini suggested that "it would be appreciated if he would send some military instruments, some trombones, tympanies, etc., etc. with the orchestration for each instrument, and several pieces of music composed for this type of group. It is incredible how the savages like music." [44]

Christmas 1845 was the midpoint of the missionaries' sojourn at St. Mary's. De Smet's glowing description of the ceremonies includes the fact that "twelve young Indians, taught by Father Mengarini, performed with accuracy several pieces of music during the midnight Mass." [45]

With the few hours left in the day, Mengarini applied the particular linguistic talents for which he had been singled out for missionary work. In addition to translating songs, the young priest set about translating the catechism into the Flathead tongue. Often far into

43 Partoll, "Mengarini's Narrative," p. 200.

44 Mengarini to Roothaan, Vancouver, Sept. 26, 1844, Mt. Sax., [illegible citation], GASJ.

45 Thwaites, *Early Western Travels,* XXIX, p. 300.

the night he would rewrite the notes he had gathered during the day, thus mastering the language and gradually compiling *A Selish or Flathead Grammar*. Rudimentary Salish vocabulary now transcribed for the first time formed the most important part of the later *Dictionary of the Kalispel or Flathead Indian Language*. He began to work on it in 1846. When he departed for California in 1852, he left the manuscript behind for the use of other missionaries.[46]

As his knowledge of the language increased, Mengarini sought out the older Indians, for as he explains, he was curious to learn from the Indians the history, traditions and mythology of their tribe. "Of their past history they knew nothing," but they would at least nod acquiescence to his questions.[47]

In 1846 Mengarini broadened his scope of Indian lore when he, along with the village factotem, Peter Biledot, accompanied thirty Flatheads and forty Pend d'Oreilles on one of their semi-annual hunts. On the one hand, he doubted the efficacy of benefit rendered by his presence, and yet he confessed that he felt moved to join at least one expedition.

Although the Indians of the Interior Plateau generally subsisted on smaller mammals and trapped others including weasels and porcupines for ornamental purposes, the buffalo hunt held symbolic and economic importance.[48] The greatest part of the Flatheads' sustenance came from hunting the sheep, goat, elk and deer

---

[46] Joseph Giorda, Joseph Bandini, and Gregory Mengarini, *A Dictionary of the Kalispel and Flathead Indian Languages.*

[47] Mengarini, "Rocky Mountains," p. 34.

[48] George Weisel, "Ten Animal Myths of the Flathead Indians," *Journal of the Washington Academy of Sciences,* XLII (1952), p. 350.

indigenous to their own area. But the horse had made feasible the vigorous pursuit of the bison to the Lower Musselshell and the Big Horn, and as far south as Fort Hall.[49]

By 1846, the elders knew the buffalo herds were declining. In fact, one old Iroquois hunter at Fort Colville reminisced in 1854 that the last bull had been killed twenty-five years before.[50]

The fact remained, however, that buffalo hides were eminently tradeable items. The sale of buffalo robes to the American Fur Company increased from 67,000 to 110,000 between 1800-1848. In the latter year, St. Louis traders purchased 25,000 buffalo tongues for gourmets around the world.[51] Furthermore, the construction of a single Indian lodge required between fifteen and twenty hides. Within the lodge buffalo meat was used for eating, the bones used as implements, the hair for decoration, the muscle for whips and bows, and the hide for endless items including kettles, boats, saddles and halters, shields, clothes and bed coverings.

With the advent of the horse in the early 1700s, entire villages became involved in this massive economic enterprise. Once in motion, the hunting caravan offered an impressive array. As Point wrote:

> Since these hunts were long affairs, the hunters took with them everything they possessed. Each wigwam counted usually seven or eight persons, and these, together with their provisions, required

---

[49] Additional information on hunting patterns can be found in Teit, "The Salishan Tribes," pp. 344-48; Ewers, *Gustavus Sohon*, p. 14; and Henry Holbert Turney-High, *The Flathead Indians of Montana*, pp. 112-23.

[50] George Gibbs, *Report of Explorations and Surveys to Ascertain the Most Practicable and Economical Route for a Railroad from the Mississippi River to the Pacific Ocean*, I, p. 263.

[51] Chittenden and Richardson, *De Smet*, III, pp. 800-07.

the use of about twenty horses. Some fifteen parallel trails, formed by dragging wigwam poles, wound between two chains of mountains which sometimes drew together to offer at close range a view of what was most majestic about the wilderness, sometimes separated to reveal a series of infinitely varied and distant perspectives. This is what was called the great hunting trail.[52]

Large hunting parties exhibited considerable organization: scouts were sent ahead and sentries were posted at night; secret communication was maintained by bird and animal cries and by sign language; messages were made by sticks and left behind for other members of the party to find.[53]

A major reason for this caution was the possible presence and predictably hostile reception of the Blackfeet. Because of their desire for the superior Flathead horses and also because of Flathead excursions in areas recently settled by the Blackfeet, the enmity was bitter. The gun and the lessons of fur trade had transformed Blackfoot aggression into an even more stealthy tactical acquisition of wealth in the form of horses.[54] At the same time, even during the period of Mengarini's residence, a religious overtone was evident in the conflict. Of this Mengarini complained claiming that to be rid of the Blackfeet was harder than dispersing a swarm of mosquitoes. From the day of his arrival, Blackfeet had regularly crept into camp by night to steal the best of the Flathead horses. "If a history of our mission would be written fully," he reflected, it would "be an account of Blackfoot inroads and Flathead reprisals."[55]

---

[52] Point, *Wilderness Kingdom*, p. 43.

[53] Harold C. Driver, *Indians of North America*, p. 364.

[54] Clark Wissler, *Material Culture of the Blackfoot Indians* (Wash., D.C., 1910), pp. 54-55.

[55] Partoll, "Mengarini's Narrative," p. 30.

Perhaps it is for these reasons that Point was to describe the Indians of the mountains as Low Britons, while those of the Plains, he likened to Parisians, cunning and deceitful.[56] Perhaps because of this difference, despite De Smet's ambitions, the Blackfeet did not eagerly respond to the appeals of the Jesuit missionaries until Father Peter Prando's work at St. Peter's mission in 1881.[57]

Additional hardships were to lead to the following description of the Rocky Mountain missions: *"Loca vastissima, aspera, pleracque"* (a place most desolate, rugged and harsh).[58] First of all the cold was such that around the layers of several blankets and buffalo robes, in which the men slept, they awoke at dawn to find robe and blankets frozen into one piece. Shortly after the house was finished, a little incident occurred which Mengarini uses to illustrate the intensity of the cold. Having filled a pan with water and placing it under his bed to warm his room as the sunlight faded at dusk, he heard "a crackling noise proceeding from the direction of the pan." Upon examination he discovered that the water was now a solid cake of ice which "rising into a kind of hemisphere, was splitting into four parts."[59]

Obviously, it was impossible to say Mass without some heat beneath the altar for the water and wine would freeze. Loss in winter of hands and feet was, therefore, often repeated in the missions' history.

---

[56] Joseph Joset, S.J., "Chronology of the Rocky Mountain Missions," ms., Box XLVIII, Jes. Arch., Gonzaga Univ.

[57] Peter Prando, S.J., "Letter from Father Prando, Missions of the Rocky Mountains," *The Woodstock Letters,* XII (Jan. 1883), p. 34.

[58] A. Salvatore Casagrande, S.J., *De Claribus Sodalibus Provinciae Taurinensis, Societatis Iesu, Commentarii* (Turin, 1906), p. 110.

[59] Mengarini, "Rocky Mountains," p. 307.

As spring replaced the heartless winter, the mosquito, equally as unwelcome as the Blackfeet, rose from the peaceful St. Mary's River. Because of the continued discomfort which resulted, Mengarini searched for a solution to the problem which reflects both humor and imagination.

> Some great-great-grandfather mosquito must, I think, have established a monastic order among them, for no Carthusian or Cistercian could be more assiduous in choir duty than they were; or he must have given them at least a great love for religious orders, so persistently were they bent on dwelling with us. More than usually troubled one day by their assiduous attention, I determined to rid myself of them. I therefore darkened my room so that the light was admitted at only one corner of the window. I then filled my room with the smoke of buffalo chips, and awaited the result. Soon, in single file, my tormentors made a rapid retreat towards the light, and left the room. I went outside to see the success of my experiment, and found quite a number of Indians drawn up in two lines and enjoying the rapid exit of the mosquitos.[60]

But hunger could not be dismissed as lightly. From their arrival at Fort Hall where the missionaries' depleted supplies were replenished with a few bags of toro, famine was not unknown. During the winter hunt of 1842, Mengarini, along with the others left behind, starved to the point of unrecognizable emaciation. A young Iroquois returning after an absence of six months asked if the young father who had been at the mission had left, so shrunken and unrecognizable was he from his diet of boiled roots. Nor was there wine for this young Italian. For daily Mass only a thimbleful was taken, since the year's allotment was but one gallon.[61]

[60] *Ibid.*, p. 198.   [61] *Ibid.*, p. 201.

Reasons for these appalling scarcities are manifold. The difficulty of communication is outlined by Father De Smet in a letter to the editor of the *Precis Historiques* in Brussels. He informed him that he had that month "dispatched a perfect cargo" of tools, clothes and provisions to Father Adrian Hoecken aboard a steamer headed up the Missouri. De Smet traced the complexity of the journey noting: "The boat will go 2,200 miles; then the goods will be transported by a barge, which will have to stem the rapid current about 600 miles." Beyond this portage, he added, there remained three hundred miles by overland wagon through mountain defiles. Consequently, "objects shipped in April can arrive among the Flatheads only in the month of October." [62]

The Association of the Propagation of the Faith, which furnished aid through the Jesuit Father General, proved to be the main material support of the missions. In both 1844 and 1845 the sum of 40,000 francs (8,000 dollars) was appropriated to the Oregon missions from this source. With the outbreak in continental Europe of the revolutionary troubles of 1847 and 1848, the Propagation subsidies began to diminish. In 1848 Father Roothaan was able to assign to the Rocky Mountain missions 32,549 francs of Propagation money, but in the following year the allocation did not go beyond twenty thousand.

Perhaps once a year did the men have contact with the outside world, and that at the cost of a perilous journey as far as Fort Vancouver which was at least more satisfactory than traveling overland to distant St.

[62] Jean Pierre De Smet, *Western Missions and Missionaries*, p. 295.

Louis. There they might receive a letter, though in three years Father Ravalli received none.[63] The goods, of course, could be transported only in good weather on mules because of the treacherous terrain.

Added to these physical limitations was the fact that the task was too great for the number of missioners, although the group was enlarged in 1843. In September of that year Mengarini wrote: "I had the consolation of witnessing the safe and sound arrival at St. Mary's of Reverend Fathers [Peter] deVos and [Adrian or Christian] Hoecken."[64] But the projects and numbers of neophytes multiplied faster than the staff.

In 1844 while on his way to the Willamette Valley to meet De Smet who had recently disembarked from a seven month voyage on the Belgian brig *l'Infatigable,* Mengarini's spirits were at low ebb. He was journeying to meet five new recruits, yet an uneasiness remained. At one point along the journey the frustration was mirrored by a departing Protestant missioner he encountered who banefully observed that considering what the Indians were and what he had, he could be of little help.

Fortunately, another party of assistants "had set out from Havre on March 20, 1844. Three of the party, Fathers Joseph Joset and Peter Zerbinatti, along with Brother Vincent Magri, reached St. Mary's by traveling overland from New York by way of St. Louis."[65]

---

[63] Palladino, *Indian and White,* p. 47.

[64] Mengarini to Roothaan, Vancouver, Sept. 26, 1844, Mt. Sax., Vol. I, Fol. II, p. 2, GASJ.

[65] Davis, *St. Ignatius,* p. 8; Hubert Howe Bancroft, *History of the Northwest Coast, 1800-1846* (2 vols.; San Francisco, 1886), II, p. 702.

On Monday, October 7, 1844, the three, along with Father Tiberius Soderini, a temporary replacement, arrived at the mission. Without guides they had journeyed to Fort Hall, and thence to the Bitterroot Valley.[66]

After the arrival of this party, the wheels of progress began to move both literally and figuratively. Among those who had accompanied Mengarini upon his return from his recent visit to Fort Vancouver was a mill-wright by the name of Peter Biledot. With the assistance of Brother William Claessens and Father Anthony Ravalli, they set to work. In addition to Ravalli's medical and artistic talents, it was soon evident that he had a mechanical bent.[67] The former system of grinding flour by passing it through an ancient coffee mill was soon replaced by the first water powered grist mill in Montana, which produced from ten to twelve bushels a day.[68]

The three also soon contrived to make a sawmill from old wagon tires twisted and bent to form a crank. Another they hammered and filed for a saw.[69] Soon they expected an abundance of planks for the construction of a new residence and a replacement for the ramshackle church.

---

[66] Bischoff, *Jesuits in Old Oregon*, pp. 41-42.

[67] In addition to teaching the basic elements of agriculture, Father Ravalli had brought with him from Europe a set of twelve inch buhr-stones, which he used to set up a small water power gristmill which produced eight bushels a day. He also set up a carpentry and blacksmith shop. Soon he also set up a drug store stocked with medicines he had brought with him as well as native herbs. Louis W. Reilly, "Father Ravalli," *Catholic World,* cxxv (Apr. 1927), p. 696.

[68] Palladino, *Indian and White,* p. 46.

[69] Bischoff, *Jesuits in Old Oregon,* p. 65.

"The afternoon for setting the mill in motion came,"
Mengarini wrote, September 21, 1845. "The whole day
passed in earnest labor, when I returned to the house in
the evening, Father Zerbinatti was not there." The bell
for evening devotions had not been rung. Even though
all the congregation searched, he could not be found
"by a hundred quick eyes in search of the missing
father." [70] By torchlight his drowned body was finally
discovered. Father Peter Zerbinatti of the Roman Province of the Society, zealous catechist and student of
languages, diminished the number of Jesuit pioneers at
the moment when the Rocky Mountain missions to all
appearances were well established. [71]

---

[70] Partoll, "Mengarini's Narrative," p. 262.

[71] John Gilmary Shea, *History of the Catholic Missions Among the Indian
Tribes of the United States, 1592-1854* (New York, 1899), p. 476; and Bischoff, *Jesuits in Old Oregon,* pp. 62-63.

A Dream Diminished

The very process of expansion and population increase, nourished by growing numbers of westward migrating whites, was to compound the tribulations of the small mission in the mountains. While De Smet envisioned and indeed pursued a policy of extending the Jesuit ministry to new tribes as opportunity offered – to Okinagans, or Flatbows, or Cayuse – Mengarini wryly observed in 1845: "There is no one to cultivate the Cayuse and Snakes who count many baptized persons among them and for all these we are all made responsible." [1]

Indeed, as Accolti was to write to Father General Roothaan on March 28 of that same year: "Our missions in the Rocky Mountains are still in embryo." [2] For this reason and for others, Roothaan did not always regard all of De Smet's reports as sober statements of fact. In this vein he once wrote the zealous young Belgian: "More than one person assures me that your relations published with so much *eclat,* are the products of imagination and poetry." [3]

---

[1] Mengarini to Roothaan, St. Mary's, Sept. 30, 1849. Garraghan, *Jesuits of the Middle United States,* II, p. 335.　　　　　　　　[2] *Ibid.,* p. 426.
[3] Roothaan to De Smet, Rome, Apr. 14, 1851, cited in *ibid.,* p. 427.

The problems of a limited staff also contributed to Roothaan's opposing the nomination of Fathers Accolti and Mengarini to the episcopacy. They had been nominated by John Cardinal Miege, formerly the vicar-apostolic of the Indian Territory. To the suggestion that the mission lands be divided into diocesan sees, Roothaan protested that at best the underpopulated areas should be administered by vicars-apostolic. No need for bishops yet.

But problems were of a political as well as of an ecclesiastical nature. By 1845, the Oregon question was an all-absorbing theme. On the one hand, De Smet commented after an encounter with Peter Skene Ogden of Hudson's Bay Company in August 1845 that: "In the Oregon question, John Bull, without much talk, attains an end and secures the most important part of the country." This led to the impression, widely circulated by Dr. Whitman at Waiilatpu, that the Jesuit papists were in league with the British.

On the other hand, in a letter written by De Smet to Senator Thomas Hart Benton in 1849, the missionary reminisces that he once warned a young Britisher on the brig *Modeste* out of Vancouver "that British conquest of Oregon and California was a dream not easily realized. He added, should the English take possession of Oregon for the moment, it would be an easy matter for the Americans to cross the mountains and wrest the entire country from them almost without a blow." The vaunt was punctuated by De Smet's proud assurance that although foreign born, he had for many years been a naturalized citizen of the United States.[4]

---

4 O'Hara, "De Smet in Oregon," pp. 257-58. It should also be noted, however, that after traveling over five thousand miles across the wilderness fron-

To the delicacy of the Society's political position could be added the complications presented by the geographic locations of its missions exactly within the disputed territory; the fact that the majority of the western settlers of Canada were of the Catholic faith, and the American pioneer vanguard were not, posed a sociological, as well as a religious challenge. Hand in hand with the opening of Oregon came an influx of whites and increase in the liquor traffic.[5] A few, like François Ermatinger, were among those traders who good-naturedly capitalized upon the Indians' love of gambling. Near the present station of Arlee he established the "Course De Femmes," where he rewarded the winners of the first women's foot race in the region, conducted on a course nearly two and one-half miles long.[6]

The predeliction toward gambling had been noted long before by Lewis and Clark who had watched Indian's lose their beads and ornaments while playing the stick game, and reported upon the heavy-betting Nez Perce, as they wagered on horse races. For this reason the missionaries viewed the whites, especially the fur traders, as a pernicious influence. De Smet had been

tier, and journeying to Europe to raise funds and gather workers in 1843, De Smet continued his involvement in western missionary work while at St. Louis University. During this time the United States government came to look upon him as its most successful ambassador to the tribes. He became in a very true sense, Minister-Extraordinary to the Red Man. In 1851 he attended the great Fort Laramie Council at the request of federal officials, and there successfully concluded the negotiations. In 1868 he embarked upon his greatest peace mission, going alone to the awesome camp of Sitting Bull. Rt. Rev. [James] O'Connor, "The Flathead Indians," *Records of American Catholic Historical Society*, III (1888-1891), p. 95.

[5] Saum, *The Fur Trader and Indian*, p. 150.

[6] Caleb E. Irvine, "Famous Indian Footrace," *Cont. to the Hist. Soc. of Mont.*, VI (1917), pp. 479-80.

quick to take measures, unanimously abolishing the
games as being against the commandments of God,
adding: "Ye shall not covet anything that is your
neighbor's." [7]

Nevertheless, the dice game was to reappear as did
the bone game in which the magic power of the human
bone being passed from one to the other supposedly
numbed the power of the opposition.[8] Gustavus Sohon,
a member of the surveying and exploration party
headed by Isaac I. Stevens, governor of the Washington
Territory, visited the Flatheads in the 1850s, and provided us with a sketch of the Indians playing the ring
game, another favored gambling pastime.[9] And, of
course, the accursed stick game referred to by Mengarini gradually reappeared.[10]

Detailed descriptions of the Flathead stick games are
found very infrequently in literature. Possibly the earliest passage concerning the form of the game was that
written by Ferris during his travels in June 1831; it is
perhaps the only detailed reference extant for the period
before the Flathead came into regular contact with the
white. In his account Ferris claimed that apparently
gambling was not disallowed by the religion of the
Flatheads, or at least it was not among the deadly
offenses, "for they remain incurably addicted to the
vice, and often play during the whole night. Instances

---

[7] Chittenden and Richardson, *De Smet*, I, p. 227.

[8] George F. Weisel, "Ten Animal Myths of the Flathead Indians"; B. Robert Butler, "Pre-history of the Dice Game of the Southern Plateau," *Tebiwa*,
II (Mar. 1958), p. 65.   [9] Ewers, *Gustavus Sohon*, p. 19.

[10] Merriam, *Ethnomusicology of the Flathead Indians*, pp. 224-236; and
Stewart Cullen, "Games of the North American Indians," *Bur. of Am. Ethn.*,
Twenty-fourth Ann. Rpt. (Wash., D.C., 1902-1907), pp. 44-779.

of individuals," he added, "losing all they possess are not uncommon." [11]

Perhaps the greatest problem, however, was disaffection. Some losses even occurred among the corps of missionary brothers. In one case, Brother Boris was necessarily dismissed after marrying a Mormon at Fort Hall, whom he divorced the next day because of her reported insistence upon Mormonizing him.[12]

Of serious concern, however, was the fact that the fervent congregations began to diminish in number and one by one the Indians withdrew from the mission settlement. Finally, in 1847, Mengarini faced an open break with a faction of the Flathead Indians led by Little Faro who had left the village and had encamped on the opposite bank with two American trappers.

The following spring brought further disavowal of the missionaries' teachings. While on their seasonal hunt, the Flatheads reverted to tribal mores, once free of the missionary's vigilant eye.[13]

In 1848 Father Mengarini gave the mission but two years more to survive. Long before, Father Point had alluded to the obstacles inherent in uniting people situated in twenty-seven different areas, making reason dominate over tribal instinct and prodding into community action a relatively phlegmatic people. To this Fathers Accolti and Mengarini added the mournful

---

[11] Quoted in Alan P. Merriam, "The Hand Game of the Flathead Indians," *Journal of American Folklore*, LXVIII (July-Sept. 1955), pp. 313-24.

[12] Accolti to Roothaan, Feb. 29, 1850, ms., Jes. Arch., Gonzaga Univ.

[13] Ravalli to Roothaan, St. Mary's, June 29, 1847, quoted in Garraghan, *Jesuits in the Middle U.S.*, II, pp. 376-77. Ravalli offers as one of the reasons for the hostility toward the priests the disappointment at the departure of Father De Smet who "had become like a brother to them." De Smet may also have upset the "spiritual balance of power" by sending Point to the Blackfeet.

fact that the best of the Indians had been snatched away by death. Perhaps, they pondered, once the salvation of these few had been accomplished the mission was to exist no more.[14]

With just lament Accolti wrote:

> The old genera[tion] of that once-brave nation, is passed away, even the good half-breed Lolo, who two years ago was attacked and devoured by grizzly bears, while hunting. What now remains is nothing but a handful of indisciplinate and corrupted youth, which cares nothing about priests and Religion, and who have no respect at all even for their chieftains.[15]

Many other reasons have been advanced to explain the closing of the mission: De Smet's association with the Blackfeet, his conflict with the superiors of the Society, and his beguiling promises of village plows and livestock which he could not provide.[16] Furthermore, in his correspondence, Mengarini points to the inadequacies and infirmities of a limited staff provided with insufficient supplies.

But of far greater significance was the dynamic force of the acculturative process to which the Indians of the

[14] John O'Sullivan, s.j., "Temporary Closing of St. Mary's Mission in 1850," in "History of the Rocky Mountain Missions," p. 186, unpublished ms., Jes. Arch., Gonzaga Univ.

[15] Accolti to Roothaan, Nov. 20, 1852, Mt. Sax., Vol. xvi, Fol. i, p. 45, gasj.

[16] It is encouraging that the open accusations allowed De Smet an opportunity to speak in his defense. On May 1, 1852, he wrote: "In the spring of 1851 [actual date was 1850] the Flathead Mission was abandoned. The why and the how I think I could pretty easily guess at. I left it in a flourishing condition in 1846; the testimonials of Fathers Joset, Mengarini, Ravalli, Point, and Accolti bear testimony to my assertion. It is abandoned five years later and I am accused of being the cause of this by my liberality and promises to the Indians, which they [the resident Fathers] had been unable to sustain. Liberal in what? Promises of what? I am at a loss to imagine." Chittenden and Richardson, *De Smet*, iv, p. 1480.

Interior Plateau had first been exposed early in the 1700s. The impact of the cross-sectional influences of the horse and the gun exposed them, as well as forced them to change. It was reasonable that these Indians would seek power, if possible, even immortality and invulnerability, in the face of these new perils. As they looked upon the first Frenchmen to enter the Spokan country of the Columbia, they designated the visitors as *"Sema,"* a word of exclamation or astonishment: "The simple Indians thought if these wonderful 'Frenchmen' came, they would die no more, etc." [17]

To achieve such ascendency over death, the Indian found it not impossible to disavow a polygamous social structure, despite the prestige that its obvious economic advantages provided to the braves. Captivated by the idea of immortality, it was also conceivable for them to attempt an epochal transformation – in anthropological terms – from unspecialized hunting and gathering to organized agriculture.

To the credit of the Society, it should be noted that in the process of catechizing and converting, the missionaries pursued the second part of a twofold plan. They removed their charges, where possible, from the onslaughts of the marauding Blackfeet and the exploitative white trader. In return, the Indian readily accepted the practices outlined by the missionary, believing that the *mana* or sacred bread of Catholicism would make him immortal. In addition to the obvious confusion over the Christian meaning of immortality, the Indians probably associated black with the color of

[17] Angus McDonald, "A Few Items of the West," *The Wash. Hist. Quar.,* VIII (July 1917), p. 199.

death and white, the complexion of the European missionaries, with the color of life.[18]

In 1847 a veteran Indian observer further explained the phenomenon which the missionaries so eagerly embraced as evidence of faith. Thomas Fitzpatrick wisely concluded that the Indians would submit to the ceremonies of "the medicine" with good grace until they found that those who had passed through all the ceremonies of religion had no better luck in hunting and war than they had had before. The only conclusion the Indian could accept was that "the white man's 'medicine' is not so strong as his own."[19] In their disappointment the priest becomes no more than an impotent herald of a meaningless creed.

In the case of the Flatheads, the Black Robe medicine was ascertained as being *itenemus* (worthless) especially after the burial of Father Zerbinatti; and as one after another of their own leaders died, some claimed from the excessive study demanded by the Black Robes. Growing disgruntlement paralleled the rising tensions at Waiilatpu the year before. Finally, in 1848 the Indians turned upon Ravalli and his medicines, accusing him of wanting to kill them in order to obtain their lands.[20]

Perhaps the hostility was a growing murmur of the emerging nativistic doctrine of Smohalla. By 1850 the "Indian dreamer" of the Columbia had urged many to

[18] Forbis, "Religious Acculturation of the Flathead Indians," p. 75.

[19] Thomas Fitzpatrick to Thomas H. Harvey, Oct. 19, 1847, Upper Platte Agency File, 1847-51, Nat. Arch., Wash., D.C.

[20] The hostility may have been augmented by the presence of whites antagonistic to organized religion in general. Their influence is noted by William H. Gray, *History of Oregon* (2nd ed.; Portland, 1870).

return to the primitive mode of life.[21] Even more persuasive is the proposition that in his years of contact
with the white, the Indian's fervor had lessened as he
witnessed the disparity between the beliefs and the
practices of many whites. The Flatheads, for example,
had received forbidden playing cards and silver coins
from the Mormons on their way to the Salt Lake. And
from their own trader, Angus McDonald at Fort Connah, they had heard laughing ridicule leveled against
all the Christian sects.[22]

Permanent settlers like Joseph Lampere and a hunter,
John Silverthorn, were soon joined by westward emigrants stopping at St. Mary's, "who made use of some
of their own to destroy the confidence and alienate the
hearts of the Indians."[23]

Thus, at the last Easter ceremony held at St. Mary's
before its initial closing, the Indians stated simply:
"You told us the religion of the whites would make us
better men, yet the whites we see are worse than we
are."[24]

No doubt, for these reasons, in the fall of 1848 or at
the latest, the spring of 1849, Father Mengarini conferred with the Superior of the Rocky Mountain missions at the Coeur d'Alene settlement.[25] The question

---

[21] Frederick W. Hodge, *Handbook of American Indians North of Mexico,*
II, pp. 602-03.

[22] "Montana's Oldest Town Was Settled Years Ago," *The Anaconda*
(Mont.) *Standard,* Dec. 17, 1889.

[23] Tom Stout, *Montana, Its Story and Biography* (3 vols.; Chicago, 1921),
I, p. 156.

[24] Anonymous, *Sunday Missoulian* (Missoula, Mont.), Aug. 24, 1941, p. 2.

[25] The Superior who authorized was Father Joset who at that moment was
serving in that capacity. Father Michael Accolti had been designated his suc-
cessor by Father General Roothaan in a letter dispatched from Rome in 1848,
but it did not arrive until 1850. O'Sullivan, *Rocky Mountain Mission,* p. 192.

at hand was the closing of St. Mary's mission of the Bitterroot.[26]

Major John Owen, a neighboring settler, took title to the improvements at St. Mary's mission for $250. In addition to the original mission built of cottonwood logs, a new structure was under construction. Around it stood twelve log houses, a sawmill, a grist mill, and several farm buildings. The understanding was that the claims to the church fields and mill would revert to the Fathers if they re-established a mission on the same spot before January 1, 1852. The text of the instrument is the earliest known record of such a transaction in the entire region.[27]

It was the formal closing of an era. Within a decade the claim jumpers would overrun Grasshopper Creek. The dream of re-establishing the reductions as first developed in Paraguay had been cynically challenged by reality. In the face of it all, Mengarini wrote: "I then asked that I might be allowed to go someplace where I should hear nothing of what was going on." [28]

The vow of obedience and Mengarini's demonstrated competence were to take him to yet another horizon on America's expanding frontier. The trajectory of events led him from Vancouver to California where he witnessed the bare beginnings of Santa Clara College.

26 Another reason for the closing, based on Judge F[rank] W. Woody's claim that Blackfoot harassment of the missionaries prompted the closing of the Mission, appears in *Cont. to the Hist. Soc. of Mont.* (2 vols.; Helena, 1896), II, p. 91. It is corroborated by Mengarini's official annual report of 1848 which stresses the immense threat posed by the Blackfeet. Mengarini to Roothaan, St. Mary's, June 30, 1848, Mt. Sax., Vol. I, Fol. VII, p. 4, GASJ.

27 Partoll, "Mengarini's Narrative," p. 66; John Owen, *Journals and Letters of Major John Owen*, ed. by Seymour Dunbar and Paul C. Phillips (2 vols.; Helena, 1884), II, p. 93.

28 O'Sullivan, *Rocky Mountain Mission*, p. 193.

Although the canticle of faith he had inspired along the Bitterroot was now sleeved in silence and his agricultural program was to be forestalled for another half-century, Mengarini's ethnographic contributions survive. While committed to the Europeanization of the Flathead, he also displayed a marked interest in the very heritage he urged the Indians to eschew. Consequently, his "Memorie" records the traditional Flathead tales of creation, and discusses their medicine, family and tribal organization and their sacred pursuit of the *Somesch*. Concerned that this way of life and its lore would be lost, Mengarini querried, listened and preserved for future ethno-historians an account of man's beginning peopled with shadowy but recognizable counterparts of Christ, Prometheus and the Angry God of Eden. He also documented culture patterns long since shrouded by passing time, and scrutinized tribal ways of a society that few, save the pioneer priest, had ever witnessed. Yet to his death in 1886 he remained unsuspecting of the significance of his work.

Part II
The Document

Significance of the Document

The significance of Gregory Mengarini's recollection is that it is more than a mere log of his work among the Flathead Indians. Mengarini scrupulously compiled an ethnohistory. Although he devotes himself to an extensive disquisition of the linguistic roots and patterns of Salishan speech, and records the death rituals and the male pubertal rites, he transcends the scientific data-gathering approach of such ethnologists as Swanton and Turney-High.[1] Mengarini's is a more descriptive style. His eye-witness account of the buffalo hunt notes the routine, the division of labor, and the method of attack, but he also records the occasional digressions and indiscretions, the disappointments and the hunger.

By strict definition the "Memorie" provides us with an ethnographic portrait of Flathead culture.[2] Mengarini's description of Flathead hospitality and friendship, his explanation of the naming of the newborn, and his unparalleled description of the process of acquiring a guardian spirit are each conveyed as part of a descrip-

---

[1] Henry H. Turney-High, *The Flathead Indians of Montana;* James R. Swanton, comp., *The Indian Tribes of North America, Bull. 145 of the Bur. of Am. Ethn.*

[2] *The Winston Dictionary,* ed. by William D. Lewis (Phila., 1940), p. 33.

tive narrative. The approach is in the tradition of the ethnographic style first employed by Herodotus in the fifth century B.C. In Book I of the *History of East and West* the titular "father of history" discusses the origins of the Hellenic race. In Book II he describes the system of caste in contemporary Egypt, while Book V traces the transmission of the Phoenician alphabet.[3]

No less a task is Mengarini's careful recording of the Flathead value system, his detailed description of the various kinds of "medicine," and his explanation of the Flathead pattern of musical composition. Clearly, the good Father has offered us far more than pious chronicle.

To this definition should be added yet another factor which gives increased significance to the document. As Mengarini describes the pattern of annual migrations, he refers to the traditional emnity with the Blackfeet, and the consequent alliance of the Indians of the Interior Plateau. Thus, to his data he has added the dimension of history, as he records the inevitable collision of the horse and gun cultures of plateau and plain. Although Mengarini does not focus upon the formulaic diffusion-assimilation of culture traits as a result of this encounter, he does provide an ample number of examples where the status-wealth symbol of one tribe was pursued by the other.

Further proof that the document is essentially an ethnohistory is provided in the chapters "Call to Religion," "Coming of the Black Robe" and "Challenges Facing the Black Robe." This portion of the account records contacts with Iroquois, whites, and eventually the

---

[3] Herodotus of Halicarnassus, *History of East and West,* ed. by Charles Hude (Oxford, Eng., 1909), *passim.*

pioneer Black Robes, and settlers with their European civilization. Although Mengarini's account confuses the delegations, he does provide hitherto unknown information regarding the names of members of the delegations. His account of the death of Old Ignace which places the burden of guilt directly on William Gray, differs appreciably from Gray's own account which excuses his identifying the Flatheads as Snakes on the basis of a well-intended act of protection. Mengarini's account of the entire history of the search for the Black Robes carries greater validity since it was drawn directly from the firsthand recollections of old Gervais and others.[4]

Certainly, the closing of St. Mary's mission, which Mengarini claimed resulted from the incursions and criticisms of white settlers, the incessant attacks of Blackfeet, as well as the Flatheads' failure to make the transition from unspecialized hunting and gathering to the agricultural system necessary to survive the onslaught of the more complex white culture, is a distressing account. But it is meaningful because Mengarini has placed it within an historical context.

The document has special significance in another sense as well. To this day ethnographers and anthropologists have had difficulty in identifying the Flatheads' place of origin, or classifying them according to culture traits. As Mengarini noted, although inhabitants of the Interior Plateau, they made semi-annual forays onto the plains and there adopted much of the Plains culture complex. As a result, in his first culture area mapping of American Indians, Clark Wissler placed the Flathead Indians within the Plains Area,

---

[4] Garraghan, *The Jesuits of the Middle U.S.*, II, p. 248, note 27.

indicating that their pattern of traits included dependence upon the buffalo, a limited use of berries and roots, an absence of fishery and a lack of agriculture. The use of the tipi as a movable dwelling and transportation over land by means of dog and travois (later the horse) and clothing of buffalo and deer skin were some additional characteristics. Most of these Mengarini clearly describes in his documentation of Flathead life. In fact, the "Memorie" may serve to greatly clarify the issue, for in Wissler's revised edition, the Interior Salish are presented as most typical examples of the Plateau group, adding that there are difficulties "in systematically characterizing this culture, arising from lack of geographical unity." [5] In 1923 Wissler's original mapping was altered by A. L. Kroeber who first placed the Flathead in the Plateau Area, and later rearranged them as an inter-mountain subgroup of the intermediate region. [6]

The origin of the Flathead, therefore, is still a matter of debate. Teit, basing his conclusions on the word of informants, speculated that they came from a territory east of the Rocky Mountains, thus falling well within the present Plains Area. [7] This contention was bitterly disputed by Turney-High, who tentatively suggested a western origin near the seacoast just below the southern boundary of Oregon. He based his position upon Flathead legend and linguistic evidence. [8] Interestingly enough, many of the long forgotten legends which Men-

---

5 Clark Wissler, *The American Indian*, p. 222.
6 Alfred L. Kroeber, *Anthropology* (N.Y., 1923), p. 337; also *Anthropology* (rev. ed.; N.Y., 1948), p. 788.
7 Teit, "Salish Tribes," p. 23 *et seq.*
8 Turney-High, *Flathead Indians of Montana*, p. 11.

garini recorded during the dusk of Indian hegemony over the Rockies closely parallel the tales of the lower Columbia.[9]

Regardless of origin, the fact rmains that at the beginning of the period of exploration Salishan settlements extended from western Montana across Idaho and Washington into British Columbia. But the true home of the Salish proper or Flatheads, until final settlement on the Flathead Reservation in 1891, was the Bitterroot Valley situated between the Bitterroot Mountains and the Rockies.[10] Its contour, composition and climate are indelibly captured in Mengarini's narrative.

A distinctive feature of the area was the abundance of natural food resources. By hunting the abundant wildlife and collecting the edible roots and berries, particularly the camas or bitter root plant, the Flathead secured ample subsistence in prehorse days.[11] Mengarini's record notes that this type of food gathering was often pursued of necessity through the 1840s.

Like Mengarini, later researchers have been perplexed by another paradox the Flatheads present. There has been unceasing disagreement as to the identification of the Flathead within a linguistic unit. All researchers place the Flatheads within the Salish language family but always with some indication that dialect differences set them off from other groups. Voeglin, for example,

---

[9] Verne Ray's studies suggest, however, that the evidence of Plains characteristics along the eastern Plateau appears to have been recently superimposed, as well as balanced by assimilation of coastal traits. *Cultural Relations in the Plateau of Northwestern America* (Los Angeles, 1939), p. 145.

[10] Garraghan, *Jesuits of the Middle U.S.*, I, p. 264; see also Johnson, *Flathead and Kootenay*, pp. 30-33.

[11] John C. Ewers, *Gustavus Sohon's Portraits of Flathead and Pend d'Oreille Indians, 1854*, pp. 13-14.

remarks that "dialect differences are especially notable among the Flathead and Spokan bands." [12] Swadeesh further emphasizes this, noting with regard to the Kalispel group (in which he includes the Flatheads):

> Taking all the foregoing facts into consideration, we deduce that the linguistic forerunners of the Kalispel group of the Coeur d'Alene must have once been neighbors of the coast dialects, perhaps living on the upper Columbia River. Inroads of Athabaskan tribes must have split them off from their neighbors and started moving them eastward.[13]

In a later study, Swadeesh approaches Mengarini's position that the Salishan language as spoken by the Flatheads served the role of a *lingua franca* in the Northwest. By enlarging his categories, Swadeesh allows for a similar inference. He speaks of the Coeur d'Alene language, in which he includes the Flathead, as peripheral to the more typically Salish groups, thus forming a separate unit. The Coeur d'Alene (including Flathead) Spokan-Kalispel, Columbia, Okanagan, Thompson, Shuswap and Lillooet are placed together in a single linguistic group called the "Interior Division." [14]

Although Suttles and Elmendorf may disagree with Swadeesh or Mengarini as to linguistic origin, their research supports Mengarini's contention that the language of the Flatheads was a reliable basis for commu-

---

12 C[arl] F. Voeglin, "North American Indian Languages Still Spoken and Their Relationships," in *Language, Culture and Personality,* ed. by Spier and Hallowell, pp. 15-40.

13 James Swadeesh, "Linguistic Evidence for Salish Prehistory," *Indians of the Urban Northwest,* ed. by Marian W. Smith (New York, 1950), pp. 151-60; Vernon D. Malan, "Language and Social Change Among the Flathead Indians" (Unpublished Master's thesis, Mont. St. Univ., 1948), pp. 23-63.

14 James Swadeesh, "Salish Internal Relationships," *Int. Jour. of Am. Linguistics,* XVI (Summer 1950), pp. 157-67.

nication north of the Plains. They summarized the
language group of the Flatheads as follows:

> Salish consists basically of two language chains, one extending
> along the coast, its center being the Georgia Strait-Puget Sound
> trough or perhaps earlier the western slope of the Cascade range,
> the other extending northwest to southeast through the inter-
> mountain interior but also following major river courses – up the
> Frazier, down the Okanagon and upper Columbia, then up Clark
> Fork and Spokane.[15]

Salishan, in conclusion, appears to be spoken in the
northern half of the Interior Plateau among the Flatheads, Coeur d'Alene, Spokans, Kettles, Okanagans,
Kalispels, San Poils, and Columbias. The only exception to the group is the Kutenais tribe which speaks an
entirely different language.[16] The complexity of this
linguistic family with its dialect differences explains
Mengarini's pronounced concern with the Flathead
tongue, devoting a significant portion of his narrative
to a discussion of it. Of course, as a linguist and author
of the first Salish grammar, he was well-prepared to
gather evidence which might contribute to a solution to
the perplexing and still-unsolved question of Salish
origin.

It is not enough, however, that the 1848 "Memorie"
be identified as accurate ethnohistory, for Mengarini's
work offers another unique facet. As he explained in his
later recollections published in *The Woodstock Letters,*

---

[15] Walter Suttles and William W. Elmendorf, "Linguistic Evidence for
Salish Pre-history," *Symposium on Language and Culture,* pp. 41-52.

[16] Swanton, *Indian Tribes of North America, BAE Bulletin 45;* Edward S.
Curtis, *The North American Indian,* ed. by Hodge; Bernard Alvord, *Report
Concerning the Indians in Territories of Oregon and Washington,* H.R. Exec.
Doc. No. 75 (Serial No. 906), 34th Cong., 3rd Sess. (Wash., D.C., 1857), all
offer detailed information.

as soon as he had mastered the language, he began to ask the people about their beliefs.[17] Only the elders were still able to reconstruct and describe in detail what they had learned as children of the Flathead cosmology. Their legends of creation, salvation, and the securing of sunlight and fire, strike dramatic parallels with the Judeo-Christian tradition. Their explanations of eternal justice, the destiny of man and the immortality of the soul are recorded in no other nineteenth century account. Although ethnologists, including Weisel, Clarke, and Gibbs, have recorded parallel legends (sometimes inaccurately abstracted from Mengarini's), only Mengarini has reconstructed an unbroken account of the beliefs of the Flatheads or the "Salish Proper" extending from what would parallel the time of Genesis to the Nativity. It should be added that although portions of Mengarini's account have been published before, the transcription which follows, taken from the 1848 manuscript written in his own hand, has eliminated numerous errors.

To this fund of knowledge, the isolated Jesuit scholar added information he had gathered about Indian herbology. Its value is greater than merely satisfying our curiosity. The account of the phenomenon which destroyed a large part of the tribe about a half century before Mengarini's arrival provides needed information regarding volcanic eruptions in the 1700s in the Pacific Northwest currently being studied at the University of Washington by Professor Richard Dougherty and his colleagues.

Necessarily there are limitations since every selector of facts will be persuaded by his predilections, as well

---

17 Mengarini, "Rocky Mountains," p. 308.

as convictions. In this case, Mengarini was burdened by two limiting frames of reference through which he viewed the Flathead. Because of what he was forced to ignore or draw into his particular focus, we have a distorted picture of the Flathead. The observer was a European and quite logically applied that culture as the paradigm in judging what he saw to be "savages," a term he consistently uses. Their economic, governmental, educational and familial patterns judged according to European criteria necessarily were seen as negatives by Mengarini.

It must not be forgotten, however, that it was at their request that the missionary came. As a Catholic evangelist, he responded to their supplications and offered the conversion they sought. In pursuing this plan, he perforce insisted that they abandon the culture patterns inimical to this doctrine.[18] Status-laden polygamy and the pursuit of the *sumesch* were pronounced anathema. Practices adopted from adversaries on the plains, the taking of scalps, the taking of the horse and gun of a vanquished adversary, and the participation in the Skull dance by the wives and sisters of the victors were all enjoined.

As with all cultures, the Flathead way of life was a web of traditions composed of a variety of accumulated techniques, institutions, and ritualized forms of behavior. Alteration of a portion of the basic social pattern profoundly affected the remaining parts. For example, the annual economic cycle of the Flatheads with its succession of movements and activities evolved in conformity with changes in local plant and animal life. The Indians shifted regularly between areas of

---

[18] Berkhoffer, *Salvation and the Savage,* p. 111.

most hunting and gathering until the agricultural pattern which conflicted directly with the Flathead migratory pattern was introduced.

Mengarini marveled at the rapid demise of certain cultic practices. No mention was made of them; instead the Flatheads overwhelmingly embraced Catholicism, fasting for days at a time and requiring the distribution of from fifty to sixty thousand consecrated hosts per year, so frequent was their reception of the Sacrament of the Holy Eucharist.[19]

At the time of his writing, he discounted the possibility that faith in the traditional rituals as well as those absorbed from the plains were held in abeyance while the "High Medicine" was being tested. The previous winter a few Flathead had encountered a large force of Blackfeet on the plains. In the ensuing battle fifty of the latter were killed without the loss of a single Flathead. Could it be possible that the religion of the Iroquois and the white man had finally made them invulnerable to the Blackfeet's savage rapacity? With the Black Robes among them, they would now know for certain. The curious absence of any reference to the sweat house, the Blue Jay dance, the Prophet dance, or the Skull dance in Mengarini's account give added credence to the hypothesis that all was being held in abeyance.

While perhaps unaware of this cultural schizophrenia, Mengarini in his later letters again avoids the opportunity to explore the sudden rejection of Catholicism during the Little Faro rebellion of 1847. The

---

19 "The Opinion of Father Mengarini Given by Letter on the Actual Temperament of the Savages of the Mountains," Mt. Sax., [no citation provided], GASJ.

Black Robes had been referred to as "men of high medicine." Furthermore, they were as white as the immortal sons of Amotkan. As they spoke of eternal life, they epitomized the invulnerability to death that the beleaguered Flathead sought. But old age, epidemics, and battles had proved to the Flatheads that they had remained mortal despite their total submission to Christianity.

In fairness to Mengarini, his appraisal of the events was necessarily distorted by a lack of historical perspective and by the fact that "not all the facts were in."

The reasons for the resistance and eventual reversion are, in fact, historical, anthropological and psychosocial. First, as has been noted, the 1830s and 1840s presented a period during which Indians of the Interior Plateau were constantly threatened and found food supplies limited by the aggressive Blackfeet. In facing this adversary the "High Medicine" – in other words, Christian teachings – had not made the Indian invulnerable. From the anthropological point of view two factors portending a negative prognosis for the success of Christian evangelism should have been considered. First of all, the weakest element, among the interior tribes, had been religion. Simple fetishism, with neither cult nor priesthood and only the beginnings of spiritual concepts, resulted in a theological vacuum in which Christianity was eagerly embraced. The white man's religion was welcomed, though, only as a cultural overlay in a society experiencing upheaval as a result of recent assimilative contact with the war-hunt complex of the plains culture.[20]

---

[20] Claude Schaeffer, "The First Jesuit Mission to the Flatheads, 1840-1850," *Pac. Northwest Quar.,* xxviii (July 1937), pp. 227-50.

Added to this instability of the recipient culture was a problem presented by both Catholic and Protestant conversion. Both religious sects saw as part of conversion adaptation to their own economic order: industry should supplant sinful idleness; farming would encourage private property and thus economic and social stability. Since both Indian and missionary viewed the culture of the other as a totality, the Indian convert to Christianity was also a convert to civilization and was forced to repudiate his own who had not been saved. In such an instance, not only did he find himself alienated from his indigenous culture and his traditions suspect, but having become truly Christian he was logically forced to be anti-Indian and thus experience a day-to-day sense of alienation and anomie.[21]

It may well be that the 1847 Whitman Massacre at Waiilatpu, with the avowed intent of killing all the "Boston People," may have appeared to be rallying round the frenzied fear that the recent measles epidemic had somehow been of Dr. Whitman's doing. But underlying the massacre, the outrages at Lapwai, the treachery of Little Faro, there was the confused protest of a society inevitably facing annihilation by an advancing foreign culture.[22] Its dedicated evangelists had simply hastened the process although the significance escaped them. Their disappointment was made more acute by the increasing number of non-religious whites who

[21] Forbis, "Religious Acculturation of the Flathead Indians of Montana," pp. 23-65; Forbis, "The Flathead Apostasy," pp. 35-40; Henry H. Turney-High, "The Blue Jay Dance," *American Anthropologist*, xxxv (Mar. 1933), pp. 103-07.

[22] Within a dozen years after the closing of St. Mary's mission, the rich gold discoveries in Grasshopper Creek had turned the area into another frontier boom town. "Fort Owen Founded Between Fur Trade and Gold Rush Days," *Great Falls* (Mont.) *Tribune*, Sept. 3, 1950, p. 2.

settled in the West. As Father Joseph Joset forthrightly observed of the Rocky Mountain missions:

We must change our customs to suit our changed circumstances. We came hither expressly to work for the Indians' welfare, and up to the present time we have had dealings only with them. In order, however, to keep our missions flourishing we ought to conciliate the newcomers. On the other hand, the Indian keeps an eye upon his rival whose superiority he cannot fail to recognize. If then the whites appreciate the missionaries, the Indians will also esteem us more.[23]

Given the fact that Mengarini was an ethnohistorian neither by training nor conscious intent, it is unfair to belabor the limitations of his recorded observations. Mengarini perhaps was not interested in associating the ritual floggings with the tradition of penance introduced by the Iroquois trained at the Catholic mission at Caughnawaga.[24] The duty was not his to study the motives behind conversion. Nor was it necessary for him to explain the gradual ascendency of women in the Flathead culture concurrent with the rise of the buffalo economy. The horse had made it possible for women to join the hunts. Since only the women were skilled at processing the buffalo for its many uses in tribal life, their presence resulted in greatly increased supply and wealth. Furthermore, the depredations of a war culture and the impact of pandemic disease had reduced the number of men and placed a greater burden of leadership upon the women.

Since Mengarini, writing in the 1840s, stood in the midst of the Indians' double-culture crisis, it would have been impossible for him to achieve a better

---

[23] Joseph Joset, s.j., "Washington Territory Then and Now," *The Woodstock Letters*, XII (1883), p. 174.

[24] Schaeffer, "First Jesuit Mission to the Flatheads," pp. 227-50.

perspective than he did. Unaware of the fact that the aggressive and successful incursions of armed Plains Indians had shaken the faith of the interior Indians, Mengarini could not have been aware of the threatened value system they now questioned.[25] By the same token, traveling with the vanguard of whites across the frontier, Mengarini could not have imagined the amount of support, economic and otherwise, the Jesuits would have had to provide in order for an Indian enclave to survive intact. Such interpretation requires perspective of time and perhaps is the proper ken of the social anthropologist.

The fact remains that the fund of Indian history, lore and legend contained in the "Memorie" has permanent value. The history of the native races of the upper Columbia, according to Bancroft, can never again be written without consulting the writings of Gregory Mengarini, S.J.[26] In another manuscript George Gibbs makes the comment: "Of the externals of savage life on the Oregon coast, there are many graphic and full accounts; but an insight into their minds is not so easy to reach. . . ."[27]

Mengarini, despite the error of some basic postulates, approached the level of insight Gibbs described. His linguistic talent, his instinctive ethnohistorical point of view and his scholarly patience have provided us with an incomparable record of a subculture in transition.

[25] Burns, *Jesuits and Indian Wars*, p. 12.

[26] Bancroft, *History of the Northwest Coast, 1800-1846*, II, p. 186.

[27] Gibbs, *Report of Explorations*, I, p. 294.

The Document

Recollections of the Flathead Mission
Containing Brief Observations
both Ancient and Contemporary
Concerning this Particular Nation

by G[regorio] Mengarini

I

The Language of the Flatheads

The Flatheads, who in their own language call themselves the *Salish* (Germanic pronunciation) and who in
Latin would be called *Selici Selicorum*,[1] are not, as it

---

[1] The Salish, a name, perhaps derived from the Okinagan word for people
which is "salst," formerly constituted a large and powerful division of the
Salishan family to which they gave their name. A more popular designation
of this tribe is Flatheads, given to them by surrounding people, not because
they deformed their heads, but because in contradistinction to most tribes
farther west, they left them in their natural condition on top.

According to Teit, the Salish linguistic family including northern portions
of Washington, northern Idaho, western Montana, a small strip of the northwest coast of Oregon and in southeast British Columbia and Vancouver Isle
once extended farther east, where they were related to tribes of that region
which he calls the Sematuse (the foolish folk) and the Tunahe. Teit states
further that these Salish were driven westward out of the plains by the Blackfeet, particularly after the acquisition of guns by the latter. Turney-High, on
the other hand, regards the Salish as rather late intruders into the plains of
the west. According to Swanton, however, the pressure of the tribes pushing
westward as a result of the migrations of their neighbors to the east as soon
as the latter obtained guns is such a common story that it is highly improbable
that the Salish escaped its diffusive effects. Hodge, *Handbook of American
Indians*, II, pp. 415-18; Swanton, *Indian Tribes of North America*, pp. 393-95;
Turney-High, *The Flathead Indians of Montana*, pp. 5-6; Teit, *The Salishan
Tribes of the Western Plateaus*, p. 295; Albert J. Partoll, "The Flathead-
Salish Name in Montana Nomenclature," *Montana Magazine of Western
History*, I (Jan. 1951), pp. 37-48. A discussion of the common practice among
Indians of referring to themselves as the "people," the "right people," which
is expressed in the word, "salish," is included in DeVoto, *Across the Wide
Missouri*, p. 10. An extensive discussion of the possible genesis of this name
is offered by Alvin M. Josephy, "The Naming of the Nez Perce," *Montana
Mag. of West. Hist.,* V (Oct. 1955), pp. 1-19.

seems at first, a part of the Kalispel and *Lkatkoms' cínt* nations.[2] Perhaps the Flathead separated from these for the same reasons as did the Pend d'Oreilles of the upper and lower lakes.[3] In recent times, for example, the Upper Pend d'Oreilles have divided into several bands as a result on the one hand of the scarcity of food, and on the other because of some arrogent tribesmen who, vaunting themselves as leaders, have gained the support of some of their nation.[4]

Not withstanding the fact that the Flatheads are frequently found in association with bands of Pend d'Oreilles, it is clear that the Flatheads constitute a

[2] A survey of recent studies would suggest a slight confusion of terms here, as well as an erroneous conclusion. First of all, Swanton designates the Kalispel or "camas people" as members of the same interior Salishan division to which the Flathead belongs. Furthermore, Mengarini speaks of the Kalispel and Lkatkoms'cínt as two nations. In truth, the latter is the name of the Pend d'Oreilles in the Coeur d'Alene language. Pend d'Oreille is simply an additional name given to the Kalispel because of their taste for large shell earrings. In summary, the two tribes are one and the same. And they are, indeed, members of the same family. Swanton, *Indian Tribes of North America*, p. 399; Turney-High, *The Flathead Indians of Montana*, pp. 278-98.

[3] Teit's contention is that the separation of some Kalispel into a Pend d'Oreille tribs is a white man's invention and has only geographic legitimacy. By the same token, Swanton distinguishes the Upper and Lower Kalispel or Pend d'Oreilles according to location. The former occupy an area in Montana extending from Flathead Lake and Flathead River to about Thompson Falls or Clark Fork of the Pend d'Oreille River, including the Little Bitterroot, southward about to Missoula and northward to the International Boundary. Some wintered on the Bitterroot and a large band at St. Ignatius.

The latter, sometimes called the Kalispel proper, are found in an area extending from Thompson Falls down to Clark Fork, Pend Oreille Lake, Priest Lake, and Pend Oreille River nearly to the International Boundary, as well as in hunting territories along Salmon River, British Columbia. Teit, *The Salishan Tribes of the Western Plateau*, p. 5; Swanton, *Indian Tribes of North America*, pp. 394-400.

[4] The reference is to the Upper Lake and the Lower Lake. The division also served to distinguish the Upper Pend d'Oreilles, who were really Flatheads, from the Lower Pend d'Oreilles. Garraghan, *Jesuits of the Middle U.S.*, II, p. 304.

nation which is separate and distinct from others speaking the same language.

Furthermore, the character of the Flatheads is admired by whites as well. So much so that nearly all of them who have lived in the Rocky Mountains for any length of time, have taken Flathead wives as a mark of status. Even the more savage nations share this admiration, to such an extent that enemy nations attempt to master the Flathead language in order to make others believe that they are Flatheads and, therefore, brave warriors. Of the rest of their history, we have been unable to determine when the Flathead nation was formed, and even less why, and from whence the Flatheads came to this part of America.

Although it does not appear so at first, the Flathead language is in truth very difficult and complicated. Furthermore, it is no way related to European languages. Consequently, for some the pronunciation is an impossibility. One might also say that brevity of expression is carried to an excess. For them one word is in reality a complete phrase. Often the Salish closely combine two, three, and four words with the singular result that the word so composed is often shorter than the simple words which made it up. This presents the greatest obstacle in mastering the language, but it also constitutes a richness in vocabulary unequaled by other languages. The expressions are truly Oriental. And when it pleases God to grant us proof, the philologists will certainly have material to study.

One might say that these savages actually have four languages. In other words that they speak in four different ways. The first is with simple and separate words as is characteristic of European languages. They use this idiom when conversing with whites in order to be better understood. The second, which is truly their language, is a laconic combination of words. The third, which might be called the familiar tongue, is broken and extremely terse, and consequently difficult to understand. The fourth, which might be called the mute language, is expressed solely with gestures. No one can imagine how impressive it is to watch two men speaking to each other with gestures, often including minute details of great events in these lengthy conversations.[5] Certainly the missionary cannot exempt himself from learning this form of communication since often he must hear the confessions of the deaf, in which case a dozen gestures will serve to exhort the penitent to do as the priest directs.

There are many who speak the same language as the Flatheads.[6] In fact, it is the *Lkatkoms' cínt,* also known

---

[5] The Flatheads were particularly noted for their adeptness in using a sign language which was the same as that used by the Crow. Teit, "The Salishan Tribes of the Western Plateau," p. 373.

Father Rappagliosi makes a similar observation, noting that "the Indians of any tribe have a common language by which they may communicate whatever they wish. It is worth noting that in sign language they are expressive to a degree beyond our belief." P. Fillippo Rappagliosi, *Memorie del p. Fillippo Rappagliosi,* p. 88.

[6] Hodge has identified at least sixteen dialect groups within the Salishan family – eight in the interior region, and another eight in the Pacific Coast region. The more closely related interior dialects include the following: 1) *Lillooet* in western British Columbia; 2) *Ntlakyapamuk* (Thompson Indians) in southwest British Columbia; 3) *Shuswap* in south central British Columbia; 4) *Okinagan* in southeastern British Columbia, extending into the United States, the subdivisions of which are the Okinagan proper, Colville, Nespelim or Sanpoil, Senijextee (Snaichekstik) of the Arrow lakes and the Columbia River below the lakes; 5) *Flathead* in eastern Washington, Idaho, and Montana, subdivisions of which are the Spokane, Kalispel, or Pend d'Oreilles, and Salish or Flathead; 6) *Skitswish* or *Coeur d'Alenes* in north-

as the Pend d'Oreilles of the Upper Lake, who speak it in a most regular and unbroken manner.[7] From this mother tongue we have succeeded in providing the Flatheads with the basis of a grammar and a dictionary which is being slowly compiled.[8]

Finally, one might say that the Flathead language is the most important of all the savage tongues in North America. With it alone, a traveler not only may journey from the United States to the Willamette, a distance of about four thousand miles, without the necessity of an interpreter. But traveling a great distance to the northeast of this mission, he will find many among the Blackfeet, the Crows, and the Crees who speak the Flathead language.[9] As a result, we might be tempted to say the Flathead tongue serves in this region of the American wilderness as does the French language in more civilized centers.

---

ern Idaho; 7) *Columbia groups* in the western part of the interior of Washington, including the Pisquow or Wenatchi, Sinkiuse, Methow, and other local divisions. Hodge, *Handbook of American Indians,* II, p. 417.

[7] Several of the reasons for this similarity are offered by Turney-High. First of all, the Upper Pend d'Oreilles, are of the Kalispel-Salishan group, and, therefore, linguistically related to the Flathead. Secondly, since the two groups lived pacifically together for centuries, their cultures blended to a marked degree, and the dialectic differences tended to disappear. *The Flathead Indians of Montana,* p. 12.

[8] The fruit of Mengarini's efforts in mastering the Flathead language are: *A Salish or Flathead Grammar* (New York, Cramoisy Press, 1861) and "Vocabulary of the Skoyalpi, Sehitsni and Salish Proper," *Cont. to N.A. Ethn.,* ed. by John Wesley Powell (Wash., 1877), pp. 248-65, 267-83.

[9] On another occasion Father Joset clearly offers contradictory opinion, observing that the Flathead language is spoken from the Bitterroot Valley in Montana to the banks of the Frazer River in the English possessions though in many very different dialects. He added, the way the Flatheads speak it differs but little. "These three tribes used much to intermarry, for they used to meet together very often for buffalo hunting. It is the reason too, that the Spokane, who used to be nearly the same, have abandoned their former dialect." "Linguistics of the Tribe," Joset Papers, Box XLIX, Jes. Arch., Gonzaga Univ.

2

The Religion of the Flatheads

To begin with, it would be most interesting and intriguing to learn about the Flathead traditions and legends regarding the creation of the world. Except among the elders of the tribes, these traditions are now unknown. Since the savage is concerned with neither the past nor the future, the younger generation completely ignores these stories. Consequently, it appears that if they are not now collected, in a few years they will undoubtedly be lost.

The earth according to Flathead legend is not a sphere, but rather a platform surrounded by water, much like an island in the middle of a lake. The sky is nothing more than a hollow mountain, or as they say, a great lid above the land and the water. Aside from this globe inhabited by man, the Flatheads believe there are many others above, beneath and around the earth.

Before its creation, *Skomèlten* (an ancient word for which was later substituted the word *Skói* (which means mother), a most powerful woman who had achieved existence independently, begot a son without the cooperation of man. This son then undertook to create the heavens, the earth, and man. Having quickly accomplished this, he then chose to live on the summit of the earth to which he gave his name *Amotkan,* which literally means: *He who sits on the top of the mountain.* Meanwhile his mother *Skomèlten* remained in another land beyond the waters.

This *Amotkan* was thus regarded as an invisible god, who according to the Flatheads, had many sons although he possessed no wife. It is for this reason that during a hunting expedition when the Flatheads saw white men for the first time, they were convinced that these were the natural children of *Amotkan,* and consequently immortal.[1] They continued in this belief until the savage Crows, at that time allies of the Flatheads, were forced to fight the Blackfeet.[2] Among the several whites who were in the Crows' camp and who joined in the battle, one was wounded and died a few days later.

Amotkan, observing from his mountaintop that man had greatly multiplied and had become most evil and degenerate, attempted to persuade mankind to return to its senses. But growing angry when man failed to heed him, he caused all men to perish in a general flood in which the waters rose higher than the tallest mountain tops.[3]

---

[1] Gibbs analyzes the etymology for the word: *Eh mooto,* third person of a verb dignifying "to sit high." This changed in composition to *Ah moto kan,* "head" or "mountain." Ella Clarke, "Gibbs' Account of Indian Mythology," p. 301, note 11.

[2] This is, no doubt, an apocryphal battle based upon the long tradition of war and outrage perpetrated by the restless and aggressive Blackfeet upon the Cree, Assiniboin, Sioux, Crows, Flatheads and Kootenay. Hodge, *Handbook of American Indians,* II, p. 570.

[3] In the traditions of several tribes of Washington, the "Deluge" was sent because of the wickedness of the people. Before the coming of the missionaries,

These mounting waters loosened an enormous poplar tree and as the flood receded, it was deposited on top of an extremely high mountain situated between the lands of the Kalispels and the Spokan, called *Chkolsm* (pronounced chekólsem) by the savages. This tree again took root and grew and it was upon this same mountain near this tree that the savages seeking initiation into the occult came until recently to engage in their fasts and superstitious dances. Last year I had occasion to twice pass over this mountain and found it truly curious to see this single poplar tree in the midst of an immense forest of pine, *lurici* and sapine trees of which this and other forests are composed almost exclusively.

After the waters had receded, *Amotkan* created other men who proved no better than the first. They were twice the size of the others and called themselves *Semtèussi*.[4] Until recently when savages encountered

the Spokanes, Nez Perce and Cayuses had their traditions of a flood, and of one man and his wife who were saved on a raft. John Eells, "Traditions of the 'Deluge' Among the Tribes of the Northwest," *American Antiquarian,* 1 (Apr. 1878), pp. 70-02.

Ella E. Clark, in her retelling of the Legend of the Great Flood, explains that it "took place long before the human race was created, back in the days of the animal people. It rained for a long, long time. The valleys were filled with water and the animals lived on the tops of the hills. Some of the animals were saved, but the big animals perished." *Indian Legends from the Northern Rockies,* p. 134.

[4] The Indians of this region speak of a number of races of dwarfs and of giants. The relatives of the disobedient *Semtèussi* are, no doubt, the giants of the Coeur d'Alene country who stood taller than the tallest tipi. The link between the two legendary figures is validated by the fact that the former were burned to death in a rain of fire, while the latter reportedly bore a strong odor of burning horn. Clark, *Indian Legends from the Northern Rockies,* p. 113.

It is interesting to note that as recently as 1930 there were reports that descendants of the *Semtèussi* tribe had come to live with the Flathead at their Jocko Reservation. Teit, *Salishan Tribes of the Western Plateau,* p. 323.

each other near some great basaltic rock, they would say
to one another: "Behold the brothers of *Semtèussi's*
arrows." Since this group of men also failed to listen to
Amotkan, they were burned to death in a rain of fire.

As a result, a third creation occurred. But because it
was even worse than the other two, *Amotkan* destroyed
it with a series of plagues. Finally, *Amotkan* created a
fourth race of men who would also have been destroyed
for their evil ways, if *Skomèlten,* his mother, had not
intervened on their behalf. The scornful *Amotkan*
finally persuaded by his mother's entreaties, promised
man that he would never again destroy the human race.[5]

Until this time there was no sun or moon, and all the
earth was immersed in dense blackness. Mankind, consequently called together in council, urged one another
to provide light for the world. But each man refused
claiming insufficient power to accomplish this. Then
Sincelèp (a species of small prairie wolf), the most
cunning and able of all of the animals, arose from the
earth and illuminated the world only a little less
brightly than the actual sun. Man was incredibly happy.

Unfortunately, however, in those days animals spoke
the language of men. Consequently, the wily little wolf
involved himself in human affairs by reporting the
secret activities he observed from on high. This met
with the disapproval of man, who in fact was so dis-
gusted with *Sincelèp's* insolence that taking hold of his
tail, which was still quite long, he pulled him back to

---

[5] The benefits of imparting the arts of life and bestowing fire upon the Indians are ascribed in some tales to *Spilyai* or *Watteetash* who was represented
as a young man, who was later destroyed by demons. Clark, "Gibbs Account
of Indian Mythology," pp. 299-300.

earth. The wolf was then forbidden to ever again create light.[6]

The crow then took the place of little wolf. But because he was so black, he naturally reflected little light. Unable to endure the heckling of humans, he withdrew, angry and embarrassed.

Finally, *Amotkan* ordered his son *Spakani* to illuminate the world. First, however, *Spakani* desired to travel upon the earth in order to find himself a wife. To this end it is said he introduced himself to the natives of the Upper Pend d'Oreilles tribe. But the savages seeing that though very handsome, he was different from them, refused *Spakani* entry into their lodgings.

Having thus been rejected by mankind, the son of *Amotkan* withdrew and quite by chance came across a nest of frogs. He joined them explaining that he had come to illuminate the world, but that first he wished to marry. Since he had had no access to the savages, he now wished to ask one of them to be his companion. One of the frogs was more than happy to become the wife of a son of *Amotkan,* so jumping upon him with one leap, she attached herself to his cheek. Thus they celebrated their nuptials. The savages seeing *Spakani* so disfigured unsuccessfully attempted to kill the frog with their clubs. Finally, the frog, more timid than the son of *Amotkan,* urged her husband to return to the heavens.

[6] Legend ascribes another philanthropy attempted by Coyote. In the distant past he attempted to bring the Flathead salmon. But, when part way up the west side of Lolo Pass, he became tired and dropped it, and it flopped back down the Idaho side of the Divide. Lolo Pass, made famous in the journey of Lewis and Clark, bears the Indian name *Tumsumcli* (no salmon). Weisel, "Animal Names," p. 346.

Immediately agreeing to this, he was transformed into the sun and began to illuminate the earth. But always attached to his face was his frog wife.

To vindicate the insult perpetrated by man, *Spakani* shrouded himself in a bright mantle so that mankind could not look upon him by day. At the edge of night, however, he would discard his mantle and rapidly cross the waters beneath the earth, reappearing with his frog wife visible to all. According to this legend the sun and the moon are the same in the opinion of the savages, the marks on the moon being nothing more than an immortalized frog. Consequently, in their language both the sun and the moon have the same name of *Spakani*. When asked how they explained the joint appearance of the sun and the moon, the savages knew not what to answer.[7]

Regarding the immortality of the soul, the end of the world, and the reward of the just and evil, the Flatheads also have traditional beliefs. For example, they believe that only half of man dies at one time. In other words, the body which they liken to a cover or a case containing the other half (unnamed in antiquity, but later

---

[7] In another account of this interrogation Mengarini writes: "then I asked them what they thought when they saw the sun and the moon at the same time during the day. They all started, looked at one another in surprise, looked up, as though searching the sun and moon, then joined in a general laugh, and covered their faces as if ashamed; and one of them, looking at me with only one finger across his eyes, said, 'Well, we were all beasts, and like enough no one of us has ever observed and remarked what you say now.' " Mengarini, "Indians of Oregon," pp. 85-86. (See Preface, note 2, herein, for variants in Mengarini's two accounts.)

Turney-High supports the thesis of the legend as reported by Mengarini, noting that the Salishan terms for the moon is "sun of the night." *Flathead Indians of Montana,* p. 23.

This may be an error in transcription. In Turney-High's Salishan vocabulary the word for the moon is *Snakokoane. Ibid.,* p. 151.

called *Singappèus*), will die, but the *Singappèus* never does.[8] The *Singappèus* of the good, journeys to rest with *Amotkan,* although not knowing what will befall him as he travels there. The *Singappèus* of the evil-doers travels to an undetermined place facing no other punishment than to be deprived of the company of *Amotkan.* By evil-doers, the savages referred to liars and thieves, for to them lying and stealing, if not the only sins, were certainly the most grievous.[9] Because of the Flatheads' abhorence of both lying and thievery (which is not found among other savage nations), they are not only outstanding, but also worthy of admiration among both whites and savages.[10]

The Flatheads also claimed that the earth and its civilization would someday cease to exist. Upon that

---

[8] Father Joseph Giorda transcribed the word *"Sngapeus,"* meaning "the soul *(anima);* the sole, lining; the soul is so called from the strict union and pervading of our bodies." Giorda, *Dictionary of the Kalispel or Flathead Indian Language,* p. 148.

[9] After spending a winter with the Salish, Ross Cox wrote the following description of their religion: "The Flatheads believe in the existence of a good and evil spirit, and consequently in a future state of rewards and punishments. They hold, that after death the good Indian goes to a country in which there will be perpetual summer; that he will meet his wife and children; that the rivers will abound with fish, and the plains with the much loved buffalo; and that he will spend his time in hunting and fishing, free from the terrors of war, or the apprehension of cold or famine. The bad man, they believe, will go to a place covered by eternal snow; that he will always be shivering with cold, and will see fires at a distance which he cannot enjoy; water which he cannot procure to quench his thirst, and buffalo and deer which he cannot kill to appease his hunger." *Adventures on the Columbia River,* I, p. 126.

[10] The Flatheads' code of morals was short, stressing honesty, bravery, love of truth, and love of family. The practice of the opposites would lead the braves to a miserable existence as "shrinking slaves of winter" in a land where fires were forever at a distance and water and game were out of reach. "Beautiful Paganism, Social Order, Noted by Fathers," *The Sunday Missoulian* (Missoula, Mont.), Aug. 24, 1941, p. 4.

last day the dead would live again, and living find themselves in a land created by *Amotkan* which would be far better than this one. After this time man would die no more.

Despite the power and nobility of *Amotkan* and *Skomèlten,* these were not the deities the Flatheads worshipped, although they certainly worshipped *Spakaní,* the sun. Being very materialistic, the savages paid little heed to that which they could not see. Thus the beaver, the deer, the crow, and other animals of all species were transformed into guardian spirits. Among them all, the little wolf was respected as the most powerful and was most favored by man. As an example of *Sincelèp's* power and favor the elders recount that long ago there lived upon the earth a group of large fierce men who mercilessly killed all whom they encountered. From their name comes the words for assassin, *Natliskèliguten. Sincelèp* so took pity upon man that he roamed the earth until he had killed every *Natliskèliguten* and had transformed each into an enormous stone. Even of late, if while crossing the mountains, the Flatheads came upon a basaltic rock standing upright, they would say to one another, "Keep aside, here is a *Natliskèliguten* petrified by *Sincelèp.*" [11]

Often during the night the howls of these wolves can

---

[11] Flathead myths reveal the remarkable familiarity with animals and nature. Even such creatures as frogs, pocket gophers and small birds, which were seldom or never used for food or decorative purposes, often have important roles in their stories. Weisel, "The Animal Myths," pp. 345-55.

The Flatheads told a curious story about beavers. They believed they were a fallen race of Indians whose wildness had vexed the Good Spirit who had condemned them to their present shape. In due time, however, their speech and status would be restored. Ronan, *Historical Sketch of the Flathead Nation,* p. 161.

be heard not far from the village. And even today there are some old women who believe that the little wolves come to warn them of advancing Blackfeet. Even more incredible, however, is the claim of some *Trochessi*[12] who claim that three howls of the little wolf heard in their village announces the imminent arrival of some stranger – friend or foe.

The sun cult to which the Flatheads were at one time devoted, is most simple. Before eating, each would take a portion of either meat or roots, and raising it toward the sun as if in offering, would say: "Sun, be so kind as to allow these animals (or roots or fruits) to grow in abundance." Without uttering more, they would begin to eat. In these matters the Flatheads were not as fervent as the Blackfeet,[13] who not satisfied with offering such food to the sun, to this day offer flesh torn from their bodies.[14] Two years ago when a band of

---

[12] As with the names of Indian tribes applied by early French and Italian missionaries, the origin may be Latin. The Trochessi may have been identified by some circular decoration or manner of dressing their hair, since the generic term for the flat circular conche shell is "troco." The validity of the interpretation is somewhat more persuasive in light of the fact a circular patty of dried herbal medicine was referred to as a "trocisco" by Greeks, Romans and Arabs in the days of the Empire. *Dizionario della Lingua Italiana,* ed. by Niccolo Thomaseo and Bernardo Belloni (16 vols.; Turin, 1924), XVI, p. 202.

[13] It has not been determined whether the Siksika received the name "Blackfeet" because they at one time dyed their footgear black, or whether the moccasins of some of them happened to be coated with black dirt or ashes from prairie fires. John C. Ewers, *The Blackfeet, Raiders on the Northwestern Plains,* p. 5.

[14] The event appears consistent with Hodge's observation that human flesh sacrifices to the sun god were not uncommon among the tribes along the Missouri. At the time of the Sun-dance pieces of flesh were cut from the bodies of the participants, offered to the sun, and then placed under a buffalo chip. Variations of this sacrifice included the cutting off of finger joints and slitting the flesh for the attachment of tongs. Hodge, *Handbook of American Indians,* II, p. 404.

Blackfeet visited the village of Saint Mary's,[15] we noticed that one of them bore a symmetrical pattern of scars upon his chest and arms. When asked how he had received these wounds, he answered that he had cut himself, adding with much gravity and devotion, that he had done it in order to nourish *Natála,* which in Blackfoot language means the sun.[16] The man was not convinced when the missionary attempted to explain the nature of the sun and of its creator.

For their particular necessities, in their afflictions, etc., etc., each Flathead prayed to the first object appearing before him, even if it would be a tree or a stone. Because of this, one of the oldest Flathead leaders recalled, when he was young, orphaned and poor, he gave way to his sorrow one day. With tears in his eyes he allowed his arms to encircle a large tree, all the while murmuring: "My tree, have pity on me so that I may become a chief, have many horses and much grass to smoke, and that I may overcome my poverty." At the same time an old blind man of nearly one hundred who belonged to the Kalispel nation, but had lived at Saint Mary's for several years, was also asked if he had prayed in his youth. "Certainly," he answered," in fact, I prayed often. Each morning my mother said to me, 'My son, come to worship.' Then she would lead me into the woods and selecting some tree ravaged by time and nearly petrified, she would urge: 'Now my son, press yourself closely against this tree and pray.' Whereupon I would say, 'Oh, old and ravaged pine, grant me that

---

15 For a discussion of St. Mary's Mission see pp. 85-113 herein.

16 If this practice of human flesh offering was exclusively dedicated to the sun god, we must conclude that *Natála* is actually Napi or "Old Man" who in Blackfoot cosmography was the incarnation of the same idea as the sun. Hodge, *Handbook of American Indians,* II, p. 571.

I may live as long as you.' I would repeat the prayer while my mother did the same nearby.[17] Then with shoulders tired and sore we would remount our horses."

Whether directed to the sun or to inanimate objects, Flathead prayers usually consisted of requests to live a long life, to vanquish many animals and enemies, and to be able to possess the horses of their enemies.

Since it often occurred, and in fact still does, that lightning kills both animals and men, it has been regarded as nothing less than an evil spirit; an enemy of the human race. The rainbow, the savages believe, is nothing more than lightning come to survey those it has killed. The Flatheads believed as the heathens still do, that the only way to escape it is to leave immediately and flee elsewhere. In fact, three years ago a tribe of Nez Perce, who lived twenty miles from Saint Mary's, quickly broke camp in the middle of a dark, rainy night and traveled many miles in darkness to escape the dread lightning.[18]

---

[17] In another version Mengarini adds: "Generally, the prayers of our Indians consisted in asking to live a long time, to kill plenty of animals and enemies, and to steal the greatest number of horses possible; and this was the only instance when to steal was not a fault, but a great merit and bravery, since no man could ever hope to become a chief unless he had killed at least seven Blackfeet and stolen twelve horses." Mengarini, "Indians of Oregon," p. 87.

[18] Such an inclemency, the Flathead believed, was caused if one whipped a snake or disturbed the rest of a night hawk. Anything red attracted lightening, and as thunder was thought to be the cause of lightening, everything of that color was concealed at the first rumble. Furthermore, the leaves of a fir called pam were gathered, dried, and pounded. When it thundered threateningly, people took a little pam powder and scattered it on the fire. The smoke ascended to the clouds and hopefully made weather moderate. Turney-High, *Flathead Indians of Montana*, p. 25.

3

Medicine Men Among the Flatheads

It is a well-known fact that every savage and heathen
nation practices magic, whether true or false, never for
the good of others, and almost always evil. Magic (the
Canadians say "the medicine") existed among the Flatheads who called it *Somésch* (pronounced [ms. illeg-
ible]).[1] And the men who practiced it bore the name of
Tlekiulsch, sorcerer or medicine man. In order to ini-
tiate themselves into this art, they traditionally climbed
to the top of a very high often snow covered mountain.
The mountain, located behind our mission dwelling,
is composed entirely of boulders and ferous-like soil
abundant in rock crystal. For seven days they remained
there, fasting, dancing, and sleeping. The animal who
appeared and spoke to them in their dreams between the
fifth and seventh days became their guardian spirit.

---

[1] The spirit of the *sómesch* consisted on any natural or supernatural entity.
It could be a bear, lightening, a lake, a flea, or a dwarf – all were equal.
Also, no spirit consistently gave the same power. Those who were given
powers had to use them whenever they were required or requested, unless the
spirit specifically stated that they could not use them. In all cases, songs were
given to the searcher, and often a fetish was left for the man. This token was
deposited in a medicine bag, and was exclusively the property of the one to
whom it had been given. Forbis, "Religious Acculturation of the Flathead,"
p. 53; *Standard Dictionary of Folklore, Mythology and Legend* (New York,
1949), p. 461.

From that time forward the Flathead initiates believed, that each time they sang and smoked, their figures besmeared with all sorts of pigments, they would attract their particular guardian spirit who would reveal his presence by singing with them.[2] He would then proceed to enlighten them, explaining that for which he had been called. Whether these spirits be false or real, it is very possible that in many circumstances the devil intervened at least in part.

Many events preceding the arrival of the missionaries, if true, make it difficult not to believe that there was some diabolical fraud. Two such recent events are worth reporting. One morning a few weeks after the missionaries had settled among the Flatheads, into their tent came Old Paul, respected by all as one of the first leaders. Because of his great age he had been baptized the year before.[3] Through his interpreters he told us that on his way to visit his horses that morning (he was going south from Saint Mary's), he had heard someone repeatedly calling him by name. Not seeing anyone, he continued his walk, until hearing himself called again, he lifted his gaze and saw a crow, which flying very close to him said, "You are going to visit your horses, for you do not realize that at this very moment the

---

[2] The connection between shamanistic practice and song is noted very early in the literature concerning the Flathead. One of the first descriptions is that given by Warren Ferris for the period 1830 to 1835. Warren A. Ferris, *Life in the Rocky Mountains* (Salt Lake City, 1940), p. 234.

[3] Long Face or Big Face, an Indian who had been left an orphan as a youth, but who had without the benefit of family ties achieved the distinction of becoming head chief, was baptized by De Smet at the age of eighty and had been given the Christian name of Paul. John Killen, s.j., "St. Mary's Mission, Stevensville," ms., Jes. Arch., Gonzaga Univ., p. 2.

For a discussion describing the first meeting with Chief Big Face in 1840 see Chittenden and Richardson, *De Smet,* I, p. 223-26.

Blackfeet are stealing your people's horses at *Squtpkein* (a place called the Gate of Hell by the Canadian about twenty-five miles north of Saint Mary's).[4] Returning immediately to warn the missionaries, Old Paul was persuaded not to give credence to the crow's ominous message.

In truth, however, the next day a young man came from the Gate of Hell to report that the morning before the Blackfeet had indeed stolen twenty-three horses. We later learned that the crow had been Old Paul's guardian spirit before his baptism.[5] The good old man, despite the crow's insistent pursuit, had renounced him long ago.

Later we marveled at the lore Old Paul claimed to have learned from this guardian spirit. Without any other study or additional effort, Paul had learned from the crow the use of herbs and medicinal roots useful in curing a variety of ailments. These herbs and roots exist in the Flathead country today, and as we will discuss later, they are effective medicines.

---

[4] Hell Gate Canyon was within the traditional domain of the Flathead Indians, who claimed the territory eastward from the Bitter Root Mountains to the headwaters of Clark Fork on the Continental Divide. Gillet Griswold and David Larom, *The Hell Gate Survey,* pp. 1-5.

Control of the canyon was attempted by the Blackfeet and Gros Ventre, whose favorite ambush localities were the narrow defile just within the mouth of the canyon and the gulch at Marshall Creek, three miles east. The resulting battles gave the Hell Gate its name. Owen, *Journals and Letters,* p. 4.

[5] Such an experience would not be considered unusual even in contemporary Flathead culture. The communication could be a formal vision quest, dreams, surprise encounters at unpredictable times and in what seems to be a relatively extended learning situation. The contact is not to be confused with experiences with spirits in the Western sense which the Flatheads view as unpleasant and unwelcome. Merriam, *Ethnomusicology of Flathead,* p. 7; Alan P. Merriam, "Music of the Flathead Indian," *Tomorrow,* IV (June 1956), pp. 103-07.

Four years ago another leader who had always behaved as well as a savage can be expected to, sadly came
to tell the missionary that for three nights he had been
unable to sleep. As soon as he would lie down he would
hear singing from above similar to that of the animals
who serve as guardian spirits to the medicine men or in
other words the shaman.[6] Since he could not escape and
was unable to sleep, he passed the night reciting numerous rosaries. He was urged to ignore the song, and to
protect himself by holding a crucifix, turning it in the
direction from which the song came. But with all this,
the voice was merely subdued for awhile. Nor was he
free of this nocturnal musician when he ordered him to
leave in peace and instead go to the missionary where
he was welcome.

The women, particularly the elderly, have also been
trained in medicine. But all their art which they acquired without guardian spirits and without much fasting, consisted in curing the ill by blowing upon their
bodies and making some gestures as if to throw out the
malady.[7] The savages, however, have been so long-
suffering and generous that they would give these hags
a horse each time they would blow upon a sick man.[8]

---

[6] Mengarini here describes shamanism in its formal sense which is based on
the theory that a spirit outside the individual takes possession of him and
that he thereafter operates only when motivated by a spirit. The practice existed not only among the American Indians, but also the inhabitants of Siberia.
Charles Winick, *Dictionary of Anthropology,* p. 481.

For Mengarini's description of the system see Partoll, "Mengarini's Narrative of the Rockies," p. 20.

[7] Obviously, Mengarini here refers to the village shaman whose two principal outward and visible acts of shamanistic curing were blowing and sucking noxious materials from the place affected.

[8] De Smet provides a detailed description of the blowing and sucking ritual
of the "doctor or conjurer" in his *Letters and Sketches,* pp. 300-01.

It has been impossible to get anything more out of their mouths regarding the particulars of this superstitious and perhaps diabolical art. They are most ashamed to speak of it.[9] What offers great consolation is that no recognizable vestige has remained since the arrival of the missionaries. But from this has developed a problem which directly concerns the missionary. Since all the efforts of the savages had been directed toward living a long life on this earth, their greatest concern was to secure a guardian spirit for themselves, and to learn from him all the secrets which would lead to a cure of their infirmities. It is for this reason that the Canadians gave this particular individual the name of medicine man. The system is universal among all the savage nations.[10] Now that they are abandoning their superstitions, consequently their medicine, which in many cases consisted *of anything but roots and herbs,* they expect the missionary to satisfy the need, while savages adopting Christianity will not abandon their guardian spirits if they are not convinced that the missionaries are much more practitioners of medicine than they. The savages, as a result, call the Catholic priests *the men of high medicine.* Therefore, a missionary who seeks entry into a savage nation without possessing medicines, or worse yet, having no knowledge of them, would have no better reputation among the savages than

9 Later ethnographers could have warned Mengarini that it is almost impossible to gather an accurate compendium of *somesch* dreams and rituals (which have often been acquired by Indians under conditions of torture). Turney-High adds that only the completely acculturized or unreliable are willing to discuss the matter. *Flathead Indians of Montana,* p. 28.

10 Others have made similar points about the Flathead vision quest, including Teit, *Tribes of the Western Plain;* Edward S. Curtis, *Indian Days of Long Ago;* Turney-High, *Flathead Indians of Montana,* p. 27.

the uninitiated to whom the *Tlekuisch* give the appellation *ikuèu,* which means as much as dunce or dullard.[11] This is so important that in areas where the Protestant ministers have long been established, the savages cannot obtain medicines without paying a great price and are consequently still immersed in all their ancient superstitions. The facts are too abundant and too persuasive to be contradicted.[12] Those [circumstances] would make me stray too far from the subject before me. Even worse, in saying it I would make queasy not only the Catholic, but also the honest Protestant, and at the same time call a blush to the cheeks of those ministers of the Gospel. Now, to finish this article, it is absolutely necessary that a missionary have some knowledge of medicine, that he have some with him, that he knows how to bloodlet. So among the articles to send to a savage mission, a copy of *The Medicine* should have first place.[13]

---

[11] Point concurred with this emphasis upon the necessity of basic medical knowledge. *Wilderness Kingdom,* p. 163.

[12] The Reverend Henry H. Spalding factually contradicted this accusation in a description of his medical work contained in a letter to a friend, Dr. [?] Allen of Kinsman, Ohio, on February 18, 1842: "I am no physician, but have more or less sickness to look after, sometimes eight or ten cases on hand at once, usually bowel complaints caused by eating bad food or too much of it. . . In the winter, however, there are many cases of lung complaint occasioned by bare feet in the wet and snow, which often terminates in consumption and death after a lapse of a few years. Blood letting is a favorite remedy among them, and I often go by the lot, opening five or six at a time and go about more pressing business, leaving them to stop the blood when they please." Clifford M. Drury, *Henry Harmon Spalding,* p. 173.

[13] Considering Mengarini's background and the period of time in which he was writing, it is reasonable to assume that the reference is to *La Medicina omiopatica considerata nel suo vero aspetto e in modo adatto alla commune intelligenza* (Milan, Italy, 1838). (Translation: Homeopathic medicine considered in its true aspects and presented in a manner adapted to laymen).

4

Flathead Customs

There is something curious about the name each savage bears in his own language. In part it is a result of the magic already discussed. With the exception of a few who were given ancestral names at birth, the names carried by the adults are not the ones given at birth, when each was named after the first object the mother touched after delivery. One was thus called *head of a bull,* another *drywood,* a third *old shoe,* and a fourth *sand,* since these were in fact the first objects their mothers viewed.[1] These names remained with the children until they became *medicine men* at which time they assumed the name of the guardian spirit who had appeared to them, and thus acquired such singular nicknames as *white raven, red fox,* and *half wolf,* and who knows what else. These they never changed except in the most extraordinary circumstances. For example, one of the most courageous braves in their tribe carries the name of *bear track* because during a successful attack

[1] The reader will readily perceive the inconsistency. Mengarini first states that the name is based upon an object the mother touches. In the following sentence, however, he claims that the name is based upon the first object viewed by the mother. Little discussion of this ritual is evident among anthropological sources since the totemic names assumed at puberty and the name of the clans and gentes within the tribe are both more permanent and more indicative of culture pattern. Wissler, *The American Indian,* pp. 174-75.

upon the Blackfeet he entered their camp to spy on their
comings and goings night after night, crawling with the
four paws of a bear attached to his hands and feet. At
dawn the Blackfeet paid no heed to the tracks, nor did
they discover the trick until they found that many
among them were dead.

Today the children receive a single Christian name at
baptism to which we add the father's savage name
according to the custom of white men.[2]

Perhaps it has already been noted that among heathen
nations, when a man dies the others gather around the
corpse during the night to chant their medicine songs.
And when burying him the next day, they surround him
with all he owned at the time of his death – blankets,
shirts, handkerchiefs, high boots, arrows, his gun, etc.,
etc., so that they may serve him during his travels in the
other world. The man's horses are also slaughtered at
the gravesite. On occasion even the wives kill themselves
in order to be buried with their husbands.[3] Upon the
urging of the whites this custom has been abandoned by
the Flatheads during the last few years. Now nothing
of the past remains but the night-long vigil during
which they alternate the recitation of prayers, especially
the rosary, with the singing of hymns as they circle the
corpse. The vigil is not only attended by the dead man's
relatives, but also by all the others who can find space in
the small tent. Here they remain until the end of the
day. If it should happen that a married person dies, the

---

[2] The baptismal register maintained by Father Nicolas Point between Sept.
29, 1846, and Easter 1847, provides examples of the Christian French names
conferred upon the converted infants. "Register of Baptisms and Marriages
Administered in the Land of the Blackfeet," Sept. 29, 1846, to Easter 1847.
Mt. Sax., Vol. 1, Fol. VIII, p. 1, GASJ.

[3] The Reverend Samuel Parker in his journal suggests that equal reverence
was extended to both sexes. *Journal of an Exploring Tour*, pp. 275-76.

surviving partner immediately sheds the clothes and ornaments he is wearing, and dresses himself in the dirtiest, shabbiest clothing he can find. These he does not change until the passage of one year when he once again puts on his ornaments and remarries.[4]

Hunting and warfare are as common here as in any other savage nation. Since we have often spoken of these practices in various letters, there are no additional particulars to include, except to say that the Flatheads' bravery and aptness in war have always rendered them as formidable opponents to their enemies, whatever nation they might be.[5] But what is worthy of admiration and demonstrates their magnanimity is the fact that the Flatheads never indulge in war unless repeatedly provoked, in which case they have never failed to victoriously deploy their small numbers against the largest enemy camps. Treachery is unknown among them. They have always had the greatest abhorrence of it, even though they themselves have often been its victims. It is remarkable that where every other savage nation after killing an enemy removes his clothing, scalps him, and concludes with a lascivious dance, the Flatheads, even before the missionaries came, were contented to take the fallen man's arms and horse, never touching his clothes, much less his body.[6]

---

[4] Even into this century the Flathead pursued a ritualized mourning period characterized by abstinence and isolation for an absolute minimum of one year. Turney-High, *Flathead Indians of Montana*, p. 145.

[5] Mengarini provides a colorful vignette of this widespread admiration of Flathead military prowess in Partoll, "Mengarini's Narrative," p. 266.

[6] The Flatheads proudly maintained that up to the early 1840s they had never shed a drop of white man's blood. In fact, this proud tradition led Charlot, Chief of the Flathead tribe, to refuse the proferred hand of friendship offered by Looking Glass, one of the Nez Perce leaders of Chief Joseph's rebel band. With contempt, he explained, "that a Flathead . . . had never shed the blood of a white man." Lawrence B. Palladino, S.J. "Historical Notes on the Flathead," *The Indian Sentinel,* 1 (Fall 1919), p. 15.

But along with these and other fine moral qualities including hospitality, even extended toward enemies; a horror of theft and lying, vices innate in other savages; generosity, justice, etc., which distinguish the Flatheads from all other nations; there reigned over them a forest of vices.[7] Among these were hatred, revenge, jealousy, insubordination, obstinacy, gluttony, gambling, sloth, incontinence, disregard for the education of their children, murder, suicide, and others we can presume of heathen savages. Recently the elders have explained to me that one angry word was sufficient reason for a woman to immediately hang herself from a tree, or a man to kill himself with arrows. As a result, the elders estimated that a homicide or a suicide occurred every six days.[8] Men generally had but one wife, but they changed them as casually as another might change a pair of shoes which hurt his feet.[9]

---

[7] Although De Smet looked askance upon the Flatheads' nonacceptance of what might be referred to as European culture traits and values, he praised their honesty, courtesy and humor. He also noted that quarrels and fits of rage were severely punished, while there is strong evidence of fraternal concern. Chittenden and Richardson, *De Smet,* I, p. 222.

[8] Although no figures are available to corroborate Mengarini's observation, Turney-High agrees that suicides were fairly common. Turney-High, *The Flathead Indians of Montana,* p. 148.

[9] Though Mengarini criticized Flathead polygamy, Turney-High underscores the dual economic and status value of multiple marriage to the Flathead. Under the sororate system, a man claimed sexual rights with his wife's sisters if he took them also as wives publicly before the tribe. As the superfluity of women increased as a result of losses in warfare and as they increasingly participated in processing the buffalo during the hunt, plural marriages also became a practical capital enterprise. *Ibid.,* pp. 89-96.

5

The Call to Religion

Such was the level of morality among the Flatheads almost until the arrival of the missionaries in 1812. They had already seen the first whites among them. But from them they received injury instead of assistance. The whites would offer them strong spirits in order to make them drunk, then they would rob them of as many beaver skins as they had. These were Americans.

Several whites who had first visited these villages as beaver hunters employed by the American company in 1828, left it to join the Flatheads.[1] They were Ignatius

---

[1] Perhaps the Iroquois arrived among the Flatheads later than 1814. According to Bishop Rosati's diary, the two Iroquois of the 1839 deputation reached the Flathead country from Canada in 1816. Ross Cox, an employee of the North West Fur Company, who was among the Flatheads early in that year, left an account of their religious beliefs and their enthusiasm for Christianity. Garraghan, *Jesuits of the Middle U.S.*, II, p. 238, note 7.

Furthermore, the actual date of migration is even more uncertain in light of Palladino's estimate which places it between 1812 and 1820. *Indian and White*, pp. 9-10. At one point De Smet cites the date as 1816. Chittenden and Richardson, *De Smet*, I, p. 20.

The earlier date seems realistic, however, in terms of an initial contact with the Iroquois. In 1810 David Thompson employed six Iroquois at Saleesh House near Thompson Falls to assist him in constructing birchbark canoes. These may have settled among the Salish, returning later to Caughnawaga to persuade others to visit the Bitterroot Valley. David Thompson, *David Thompson's Narrative of Explorations in Western America, 1784-1812*, ed. by J. B. Tyrrell (Toronto, 1916), p. 418.

called the *Large,* Peter and another Ignatius called the
Small to distinguish him from the first. All three were
Iroquois, and called whites simply because they spoke
French. With them was an aged Canadian called Jean
Baptiste Gerve, as well as a creole.[2] Each was a Cath-
olic.

When they had mastered the essentials of the savage
tongue, they began telling thousands of things about the
customs of the white settlements. They also gave the
Flatheads their first instructions regarding the true God
and our Holy Religion. From then on the Flatheads
began to distinguish good from evil. Ignatius the Large
could be considered the first the Lord used to dispel the
murky darkness that until then had shadowed the minds
of our savages. His words along with his honest conduct, characteristics most difficult, and I would say
almost impossible to find among whites who live with
the savages, appealed to the hearts of many, especially
the elderly who passed not only days but often entire
evenings in the tent of this precursor, so to speak, in
order to hear him speak of God and of his religion, but
above all about Baptism.

It was then that the Flatheads heard reference made
to certain white men dressed in black who instructed
people in the knowledge of God and all good things and
who made man live after death. Whenever Ignatius
spoke with the savages (Old Gerve recently observed),

---

[2] When referring to the Creole, Mengarini was undoubtedly designating
Gabriel Prudhomme, a mixed blood, but an adopted child of the Flathead
nation. He was the first to meet the missionary contingent on the banks of the
Green River. Subsequently he was often to serve as interpreter for the missionaries. Chittenden and Richardson, *De Smet,* I, p. 292.

Jean Baptiste Gerve is Jean Baptiste Gervais in Garraghan, *Jesuits of the
Middle U.S.,* II, p. 238, note 8.

he usually ended by saying, "And my friends all that I say is nothing. If those dressed in black should come here they would know, for it is from them that I learned all of this which I tell you." The Flatheads wished that Ignatius would teach them some prayers, but this he steadfastly refused for fear of changing the words of God.

By a fortuitous act of Divine Providence, the efforts of Ignatius the Large aroused in the Flatheads a great desire to have such men among them. But they did not dare speak, not knowing what to do to obtain them. One day when as usual Ignatius was engaged in religious conversation with them, the Flatheads asked, "Why do not those Black robes of whom you so often speak also come among us?" Ignatius did not let this question pass, but immediately answered, "And you. Why do you not seek them? You will find them in the lands of the *Soiapi* (the Americans) and I am certain that they would come if you would but seek them." At which point he turned to the chief, who at this time was Old Peter (who died in 1841 and of whom we spoke in letters written that same year), and implored him to send some representatives of his tribe to St. Louis in search of Catholic missionaries. As a result, he dispatched four Flatheads on this mission in the spring of 1830. Along with three Nez Perce they safely reached Independence, a city located along the United States frontier about three hundred and fifty miles from St. Louis.[3] But when they attempted to resume their trip after

---

[3] The actual distance between Independence and St. Louis is 224 miles but following the meanderings of the Missouri River at that point would make the distance considerably greater. J. Paul Goode, *Goode's World Atlas* (10th ed.; Chicago, 1957), p. 79.

remaining there for several days, they all fell ill. Within
a few days two Flatheads and two Nez Perce died. The
other three losing heart turned back. During the journey the remaining Nez Perce died, and the two Flatheads returned to their tribe having achieved nothing
by their expedition.

Although the Flatheads were disappointed to say the
least, stouthearted Ignatius the Large announced to all
that he himself would go. This he did two years later.

But before this second expedition two noteworthy
events occurred in the Flathead village. Information
regarding the [Flathead] expedition had not only been
received by Monsignor Rosati, bishop of St. Louis, but
also by the fathers of our own company, and most probably also by Protestant missionaries. Consequently, one
day during the spring following the expedition, a Protestant minister appeared before the Flatheads and their
allies the Nez Perce with whom they were encamped.
Convening all the men of the two nations together and
placing himself in the center, he announced that he had
come to instruct the savages and to remain with those
who chose to keep him. Ignatius the Large, who had
already explained to the Flatheads the difference between the Catholic missionaries and the Protestants,
remained to hear what his followers would say. But
they did not show themselves eager to answer. After
all, the minister had already indicated his willingness
to remain with the Nez Perce, who noting the silence of
the Flatheads, accepted him among themselves. Ignatius
the Large was so pleased with the behavior of the
Flatheads that after the assembly was dismissed, he
embraced one after the other thanking them for con-

ducting themselves so well, and promising that he himself would go in search of the Black Robes.

In the autumn of that same year it also befell that a
young savage of the Spokan tribe who several years
before had been taken by the American to be educated
in the United States, returned or rather was returned
to his own people with instructions to minister to the
savages of all the adjacent tribes.[4] Since he feared that
because of his youth he would not succeed, his father
assumed the burden of this important mission, not hes-
itating to communicate to all the allied nations the great
knowledge which his son had received from the Americans. Unfortunately, he appeared among the Flatheads
during the absence of Ignatius the Large who was then
living with the Snakes.[5]

Thus he fervently began to preach to the Flatheads
from morning till night, saying that from his son who
had returned from the lands of the Americans, he had
learned that it was true that after death there was
another life. But that to achieve it, it was absolutely
necessary to have *at least* two wives, that all good whites

[4] This could be a reference to the sending of two Spokan boys, Pelly and
Garry, and later others to the Red River settlement and school of the Hudson's
Bay Company. Drury, "Oregon Indians of the Red River School," p. 53.

On the other hand, the mention of the United States suggests the return of
two Spokane Indians in the company of Dr. Marcus Whitman to upstate New
York in 1835. "Annals of Kansas," pp. 45-46. This is supported further by
Hafen and Ghent's observation regarding the 1835 homeward journey under-
taken by Dr. Whitman and two Indian boys in the company of Thomas
"Broken Hand" Fitzpatrick. Hafen and Ghent, *Broken Hand,* p. 116.

[5] During his visit to St. Louis De Smet reported to Father Ferdinand Helias,
s.j., the display of religious fervor he had witnessed: ". . . there were
seven nations who had asked him to bring them a priest," De Smet explained,
"namely, the Flatheads, Onapersé [Nez Perces], Panthéres [?], Coltonais
[Kutenai], Lespokans [Spokan], Cajous [Cayuse], Ochazeres [?], in all about
6000 souls." Garraghan, *Jesuits of the Middle U.S.,* II, p. 247.

who wished to save themselves did thusly. Furthermore, they should be careful not to allow into their lands certain men dressed in black *having no wives,* because they were very clever and also dishonest. To the Americans alone could they entrust themselves. Heeding them, they would be saved. But those who pursued the creed of the Black Robes would be irredeemably consigned to the fire. They should also be aware of the many evils committed by these Black Robes. For example, when a man died they pretended to bury the body in a wooden casket displayed before the people. But in reality they ate him. This they did with all their dead. In the United States when a Black Robe attempted to bury a body, the Americans threw themselves upon the casket, breaking it into pieces. Instead of finding the corpse within, they found a coffin filled with sand. These and many other great doctrines and revelations were the standard theme of this herald of Satan. This demonstrated to the Catholic missionaries how much the enemy of good worked to prevent the propagation of Christ's reign upon earth, and to retain in his infernal clutches the souls which he had so long held in his possession.

In the meantime the elder Spokan, not satisfied addressing the people as a congregation, often entered the individual tents of the savages to further persuade each to conform to the doctrine of the *enlightened whites.* He even urged the leaders to acquire three women so that they would be even more uplifted. This diabolical strategy made an immense impression upon the minds of a large part of the tribe. Believing all which this emissary of infernal propaganda uttered, particularly with regard to polygamy, the Flatheads surrendered to his persuasions. A few men of good sense, almost all of whom were chiefs, and the people who had most faithfully attended Ignatius's instructions refused, however, to submit to the Spokan and persisted with constancy in their monogamy. Thus they were forced to endure the ridicule of this manifest demon.

From them we have learned the facts and heard the criticisms and evil spoken against the Catholic missionaries and their religion, as well as hearing of the praise for the Americans and their easy, benevolent religion. The Spokan had already departed when Ignatius the Large returned to the Flatheads, and by the greatest providence of God, the Creole, of whom we have spoken, accompanied him. Since he was an American, he could dismiss the many lies advanced by that scoundrel Spokan. Ignatius the Large often employed him to dissuade the Flatheads from this new system they had adopted. But the evil had already established a foothold.

As a result, a kind of schism was formed at that time. The Flatheads divided into two religious groups, one calling itself the Followers of Ignatius the Large and the other, the Followers of the Spokan. Thus they remained until the arrival of the missionaries about nine years after this infernal machination.

Ignatius the Large then resolved to go himself to the United States, and not to stop until he had reached the feet of the Monsignor Bishop to ask for missionaries. In fact, the following spring he began the journey in the company of three Flatheads, one American, and one Nez Perce. They were well along on their journey when Ignatius the Large discovered tracks apparently belonging to the Sioux, a group to whom he could not prudently entrust himself. When he attempted to leave the trail, however, in order to avoid them, the American insisted that they not make a detour. They traveled no more than a mile, however, before they encountered the members of the entire Sioux camp, who running in groups and shouting according to their savage custom, forced the small band to a halt. One of the chiefs asked the American to which tribe his companions belonged. He, we know not for what end or intention, answered that they were all Snakes. The chief then advising the American and Ignatius to stand aside, fell upon the Indians in order to kill them. Ignatius, however, was not as civil as his American mentor, and he leaped to the defense of his companions. But in a few moments all were killed, and the American, in spite of the fact that he was to one side, received a bullet in his head and fell unconscious, immersed in his own blood. He learned at his own expense that a lie is never profitable. While the corpses were being stripped, the American regained consciousness and claimed that the slaughtered Indians were not Snakes but Flatheads. Upon learning this the Sioux were so filled with remorse that they were on the verge of slaying the American until one of their chiefs declared that having attempted to kill him once, they should not try again. They thus allowed him his life, and he eventually returned among the Nez Perce where he now lives, bearing the shame and remorse of having caused the death of innocent men with a lie. Thus did Ignatius the Large offer his life for the sacred cause of religion and as a martyr to charity.

His son Francis, a youth of twenty-four who for

many years served as interpreter for the missionaries,
walks in his father's footsteps, always loyal to the faith
and most attached to the missionaries, a hardworking
man and an example to the savages.[6] Not withstanding
the freshness of his age, he has already offered proof of
his constancy and extraordinary magnanimity despite
the fact that his father was slain by the Sioux and last
year his mother was killed by the Blackfeet. His wife
died this winter. His three children died a year after
their baptism, and he himself remained suspended
between life and death for five weeks. In addition to
these calamities, the Blackfeet have robbed him of his
horses for which he had paid his entire savings.

[6] In 1903 Francois Xavier Saxa (meaning Iroquois), also known as Francois
Lamousse, the son of Big Ignace who had accompanied his father to St. Louis,
was still living near Arlee, Montana. Chittenden and Richardson, *De Smet*, I,
p. 292, note 3.

6

The Coming of the Black Robe

The Flatheads much saddened not only by the failure of the first two expeditions,[1] but also at losing the assistance and counsel of a man from whom they had received the seeds of Christian morality, thought no more of undertaking an expedition. But since God had not challenged their faith without intending to reward them later with more abundant graces, He thus inspired the other two Iroquois, Peter and Ignatius the Small, to try again. They discussed the project with the chief, stressing that they desired no native companions. Good and prudent Peter had already developed a plan and had decided not to undertake such a trip without being absolutely certain of at least reaching St. Louis. Since the sad experience of his predecessors had shown him that it was dangerous to stop on the way, once within the confines of the United States and even more dangerous to travel in small numbers, he decided not to pause

---

[1] Mengarini apparently confuses the various Flathead delegations. Actually, they were four in number as is correctly stated by De Smet. Chittenden and Richardson, *De Smet,* I, p. 290; Garraghan, *The Jesuits of the Middle U.S.,* II, p. 238, notes 7 and 8; a fuller version of the account is found in Palladino, *Indian and White in Northwest,* pp. 237-38, 242-50; George Finnegan, S.J., "Quest of Indians for the Blackrobe," *The Tablet* (n.d.), Jes. Arch., Gonzaga Univ.

en route unless in the company of a strong brigade and never to stop in a city encountered in passing because of the diseases prevalent in these settlements.

A propitious opportunity presented itself in 1839 when a large company of American beaver hunters, who had been living for sometime in the native villages, passed through on their way to the United States.[2] Peter, Ignatius, and a young Nez Perce joined the group and arrived hale and hearty in St. Louis at the end of autumn.[3]

On behalf of the Flatheads they requested missionaries of Bishop Rosati and of the provincial representative Verhaegen.[4] In the following spring they were assured that a Father of the Company would visit them. Ignatius remained at the novitiate of Florissant throughout the winter, and later became the guide and interpreter of Rev. P[eter] De Smet.

Peter, seeing that he had achieved all the desired objectives, hesitated no more in exposing himself to danger: he carried the happy news to the Flatheads. With no companion but the Nez Perce, and with no provisions, he departed immediately. Although it was necessary to travel all winter, he was undaunted by the danger of dying from hunger and cold. In order to

---

[2] Peter Gaucher (Left-hand Peter) and Young Ignace who formed the fourth delegation left home in the summer of 1839. According to Palladino, they joined a group of Hudson's Bay Company men about to make the voyage to St. Louis by canoe. Their course most naturally lay down the Yellowstone and Missouri rivers. In passing St. Joseph's Mission, at Council Bluffs, they stopped to confer with the priest in charge and by remarkable coincidence met Father De Smet. *Indian and White in Northwest,* p. 27.

[3] See p. 35, herein.

[4] Peter Joseph Verhaegen was the first president of (new) St. Louis College, 1829-1836, and vice-provincial of the Missouri mission and vice-province from 1839 to 1843. Davis, "Years of Preparation," p. 183, note 48.

avoid falling into the hands of savages they were forced to pass, the two often detoured from the regular route and frequently were lost. The Nez Perce could not long sustain the hardships of the trip; consumed by exhaustion and hunger, he died.

Peter continued his journey living on an occasional wild root which he pulled with difficulty from the frozen, snow-covered ground. Soon after, his horse also perished. Peter now found himself alone and on foot, without any provisions to sustain life, and still a great distance from the Flathead village. Although he had a gun, he had been so reduced by haggard exhaustion that he no longer possessed the strength to hold it to his shoulder. Pursuing the animals in order to slay them was even more out of the question. In April, as a result of God's protection, he finally reached the Flatheads, barefoot, almost naked, and so transformed that he was hardly recognizable.[5] Overjoyed and ignoring his condition, and before taking food as is the usual savage custom, he reported that the heads of the Black Robes had listened to his requests and that Ignatius had been retained in order to return shortly with the missionary. In fact, in the summer of that same year, 1840, Rev. P[eter] de Smet joined the Flatheads who were then in the midst of their buffalo hunt.[6]

---

[5] Peter arrived at Eight Mile Creek in the Bitterroot to announce the good news at about the time that Father De Smet left St. Louis, Mar. 27, 1840, with young Ignace on his way to the Rockies. "Left-Hand Peter's Hazardous Winter Journey With News," *Sunday Missoulian* (Missoula, Mont.), Aug. 24, 1941, p. 2.

[6] Father De Smet arrived with a staff for a permanent mission on Aug. 15, 1841. Shea, *Church in the United States,* (4 vols.; New York, 1886-1892), III, p. 313.

7

The Lands of the Flatheads

Perhaps it would be appropriate here to summarize the views of the Fathers, derived from their letters written up to and including the year 1847, respecting their comments on the life of the savages living at St. Mary's.[1]

The village of the Flatheads and the residence of the missionaries are located on a large plain shaped like an oval, a basin about fifty miles in length, at some points six miles wide and at others eight or ten.[2] Two great

---

[1] Preface, note 1, herein. Additional letters are located in GASJ and on microfilm in the Jes. Arch., Gonzaga Univ.

[2] The homeland of the Flathead tribe proper, at least in historic time, was just west of the Continental Divide in the Bitterroot Valley. Teit, "Salishan Tribes," p. 310; Turney-High, *Flathead Indians*, p. 12. Here they were found by Lewis and Clark in 1804. The dearth of archeological evidence raises the question, however, of how long the region has been occupied. Johnson, *Flathead and Kootenay*, p. 29.

The valley has, as De Smet notes, "but one fine defile, the Hell Gate, offering issue and entrance to the valley." Chittenden and Richardson, *De Smet*, I, p. 344. This was a fact of unusual consequence to a people continually harassed by the more powerful and numerous Blackfeet and Crows who lived east of the Rockies.

In the Missoula Valley to the northwest of Hell Gate gorge was an established assembly ground where many tribes and the whites met one another for affairs of peace and white traders came to exchange their goods. To the west of the Bitterroot Valley, and extending for its entire length, stood the formidable barrier of the Bitterroot Mountains, nearly two hundred miles long from north to south and having a width of from fifty to seventy-five miles. This tremendous tumult of peaks constitutes what is perhaps the most difficult area

chains of mountains which are almost always snow-
covered border the plain from north to south. Their
height above sea level is such that they could be described as forming the backbone of the earth's crust in
this region.[3] The river flowing by the village, which is
a branch of the Columbia River, disappears about forty
miles to the southeast of Saint Mary's. Near there
emerge the headwaters of the Missouri.[4] The first is
twelve hundred miles from its mouth on the Pacific
Ocean, unnavigable due to rapids and falls from Saint
Mary's to Vancouver. The other is four thousand miles
from the Gulf of Mexico.[5]

Its great elevation above sea level is probably the

---

of equal size within the continental limits of the United States, and it is still,
in parts, virtually unknown and unpenetrated. The only practicable pass
through these mountains is the Lolo, which debouches from the valley about
ten miles from its lower or northern end. Some fifty miles south of the Lolo
Trail the lofty Nez Perce Pass also leads to the westward, but no war party
could successfully attack the Flatheads by that route. Further southward,
where the Bitter Root merges with the mainstream of the Rockies are several
other minor passes but they are nearly impassable. Owen, *Journals and Letters,* I, p. 4.

[3] To the west Mengarini refers to the Bitterroot Range; east he alludes to
the Lewis Range of the Big Belt Mountains. Goode, *World Atlas,* p. 73.

[4] The Bitterroot River, or as De Smet called it, the St. Mary's River, rises
in two forks in the main chain of the Rockies, on the northern slope of the
divide between Montana and Idaho, and flows almost directly north through
a beautiful, fertile valley eventually emptying into the Columbia by way of
the Clark Fork and Pend O'Reille rivers. To the east of the Divide tributaries
join to form the Missouri River.

David Thompson did not realize that the northward-flowing river he came
upon June 30, 1807, was the source of the Columbia. Instead he named it the
Kootenae in honor of the inhabitants of the surrounding prairie. David
Thompson, "Discovery of the Source of the Columbia River," *Oreg. Hist.
Quar.,* XXVI (Mar. 1925), pp. 23-49.

[5] In reality the aerial distance between St. Mary's and the Mississippi delta,
the logical point of definition along the Gulf, is 1700 miles. Although such
measurement does not allow for the meandering course of the river, it indicates that the distance would still be somewhat less than 4,000 miles.
C[harles] S. Hammond, *Hammond's Globemaster World Atlas* (New York,
1948), p. 38.

reason for the infrequent rainfall in this village, as well as the reason for the frosts which continue not only into spring and autumn, but into summer which itself is limited to the months of June and July. There is little doubt, furthermore, that the great elevation accounts in part for the truly terrible storms which at times continue for entire weeks without cessation.[6] These three things, the lack of rain, the cold, and the storms, make the village most unpromising for farming.

The soil, which is naturally dry and filled with large rocks, becomes even less fertile because of the draught, and we cannot find arable spots except along the creeks which are often located great distances from each other. We can have some idea of the difficulty this presents when we consider that to cultivate one hundred acres of land the Flatheads are forced to make five different camps within a sixteen mile area. In addition to this, the large rocks hidden beneath the surface of the ground frequently break the plows, rendering them useless. The cultivation of the land is further curtailed by the frost which continues throughout the year. With the exception of wheat, barley, oats, and a few potatoes, we have been unable to harvest much.[7] We have succeeded

---

[6] The influence of elevation cannot be disputed. In a geographic range where winter temperatures in January average 10° to 30° above zero, the Cordillerian Plateau temperatures are much lower. Goode, *World Atlas,* p. 8.

[7] De Smet offers a conflicting observation in a letter written September 6, 1846. Discussing the agricultural progress at St. Mary's, he observes: "The soil yields abundant crops of wheat, oats, and potatoes – the rich prairie here is capable of supporting thousands of cattle." Thwaites, *Early Western Travels,* XXIX, p. 322.

Like De Smet, Father Adrian Hoecken was optimistic, writing: "Our Indians do very well, we have about a 100 bushels of wheat, barley, peas, corn, potatoes, in the ground. St. Mary's mission, according to Indian relations, has produced more than will be consumed – the saw and grin(d) mill are in operation." Adrian Hoecken to Father Superior Joseph Joset, St. Ignatius, May 10, 1845, GASJ.

in growing no legumes except for peas. Unfortunately, these and the wheat, which could yield much nourishment, are completely destroyed in the bloom of their growth by storms, causing those who come to this country to apply to themselves the biblical condemnation: *In sudore vultus tui vesceris pane.*[8]

All the Flathead lands abound in a wide variety of herbs, principally *artemisa* or *Ormoise estragon.*[9] We also find *angelica* which is used as a headache remedy by the savages who grind the roots and then inhale the powder through the nose;[10] and gentian *lutea purpurea* and *chirayta,* the leaves of which are potent poison, especially for horses who die a few hours after eating it.[11] Consequently, the savages, though having great knowledge of these roots, fear them. Other herbs are:

---

[8] The passage is more familiar in translation: "In the sweat of your brow you shall eat bread. . ." Genesis 3:19.

[9] *Ormoise estragen* may have been Mengarini's French appellation for *artemisia dracunculus,* known in English as tarragon. The herb found in central and southern Europe, Russia and Siberia has the following applications: appetizing, stomachic, diuretic, aromatic, cooling, carminative, antiscorbutic, emmenagogue, vermifuge, used for culinary purposes. Edward F. Steinmetz, *Codex Vegetabilis* (Amsterdam, 1957), No. 138.

[10] The abbreviated reference does not indicate clearly whether the herb in question was *angelica silvestris,* which is indigenous to temperate areas and more bitter in flavor than *angelica archangelica* or *archangelica officinalis.* Since both can serve as nerve tonics and antispasmodics, the Flatheads could have used both for a headache remedy. The fact, however, that the latter grows as far north as Lapland and Iceland suggests that it may have been the *angelica* of Montana. *Ibid.,* No. 157.

[11] Because of the profuse growth of *gentian lutea* or bitterroot in their valley the Flatheads thus named the valley and the surrounding mountains. Gentian has been known from the days of antiquity, and included in many complex remedies handed down by the Greeks and the Arabs. The curative quality of the bitter gentian is limited to a local effect upon the mucous membrane of the alimentary tract. The only justification for Mengarini's assertion as to the poisonous qualities of yellow or purple (Indian) gentian would be that an overdose would act as a local irritant causing nausea. Arthur Osol, Robertson Pratt, and Mark D. Altschule, *The United States Dispensatory and Physicians' Pharmocology* (26th ed.; Phila., 1967), p. 538.

agrimonia officinale, of which the natives use the roots, not the leaves, as antidotes for diarrhoea and sore throat;[12] *apium graveolensor* or wild celery which the Flatheads and other savages in this part of North America smoked before learning of tobacco;[13] *cicuta maculata,*[14] *cicutaria quatica* or *cicuta virosa*[15] which in an extraordinary quantity causes death not only among animals, but also among the natives themselves, especially the children, if they are not forced to swallow great quantities of liquified fat. Finally, there are *cochlea via armoracea, la digitale pupurea* and *camomila,*[16] as well as a great number of other herbs and

[12] *Agrimonia officinale* may refer to the liverwort plant, officially known as *agrimonia eupatria.* The herb, found in Europe, northern Asia and North America, is useful as a diuretic, astringent and in treating enurisis nocturna. Steinmetz, *Codex Vegetabilis,* No. 41.

[13] *Apium graveolensor dulce* is found almost throughout the world and is described as an aromatic seed used as a diuretic, carminative, and emenagogue. Steinmetz, *Codex Vegetabilis,* No. 111. Its value as an alternative to tobacco is unique to the North American Indians. Of this later predilection for tobacco, Ross Cox writes: "They [the Flatheads] were passionately fond of tobacco, and while they remained with us never ceased smoking." *Adventures,* p. 102.

[14] *Cicuta maculata* or poison hemlock and *cicutaria quatica (cicuta aquatica),* also known as cowbane or water hemlock, are entirely poisonous, especially the hollow roots which are often mistaken for parsnips. A single mouthful can kill a man within fifteen minutes. Wyeth Laboratories, *Sinister Garden* (New York, 1966), p. 36.

[15] *Cicuta virosa,* less common than the water hemlock, appears similar to the untrained eye. The poisonous properties are the same. The brown, resinlike substance, cicutoxin, is the most violent poisonous species in the United States. Children and adults have found the root fatal, though greatest mortality has been among cattle. But during the spring, when it is believed the plant is most poisonous, even horses, sheep, and swine have died. Walter Muenscher, *Poisonous Plants of the United States* (Rev. ed.; New York, 1951), p. 175.

[16] *Cochlearia armoracia* or horseradish is used as both a stimulant and as an appetizing aid to the digestive process. Steinmetz, *Codex Vegetabilis,* No. 325.

Digitalis purpurea or purple fox glove was named after its finger-shaped corolla by Tragus in 1539. The plant is a biennial herb, probably indigenous

roots which the savages often use, but which we are
unable to name, for the savages gather them far from
Saint Mary's. I have also noticed a kind of white carrot
which presumably is similar to the white carrot of
Silesia. The savages make little use of it, however,
because its sweet flavor disgusts them.[17]

The mountains are composed of aggregate granite
which is particularly well adapted for millstones.
Within one hundred and fifty miles of St. Mary's I
detected not one indication of limestone, or chalk, or
coal, not to mention a variety of minerals.[18]

Without a sextant it is impossible to determine the
geographical location of our mission with any great
degree of exactitude. According to many maps, however, we can calculate the location as being approx-
imately between 117° and 120° longitude and between
46° and 47° latitude.[19] Nevertheless, the cold is exces-

to central and southern Europe and naturalized in various parts of Canada,
Europe and the United States. It has been official in most pharmocopeias since
the eighteenth century. Edward P. Claus and Varro E. Taylor, *Pharmocognosy*
(5th ed.; Phila., 1965), p. 96.

Camomila, common camomile or *matricaria chamomilla,* is a widely available flowered herb used as a sedative, antiseptic, digestive tonic and soporific.
Steinmetz, *Codex Vegetabilis,* No. 698.

[17] This may be similar to the "small white root of rather insipid taste," referred to by Gibbs, *Report of Explorations,* p. 193.

[18] Mengarini did not suspect the area possessed great mineral wealth. Copper, lead, silver and coal were later found in extensive deposits. Stout, *History
of Montana,* I, pp. 101-02. The region also contained deposits of pipe clay
which the Flatheads used regularly to clean their leather shirts and robes.
Nineteenth century observers also noted that the Flatheads conducted a brisk
trade in objects made from the flint and pipestone secured in quarries on the
upper limits of Flint Creek flowing through Hell Gate Canyon. Ronan, *Historical Sketch of the Flatheads,* p. 9. They were also famous for fine pipes of
black stone inlaid with Catlinite and other materials found in the Flathead
country. Wissler, "Material Culture of the Blackfoot," p. 83.

[19] Mengarini's computations are accurate in view of his limited resources
for gathering data. Present-day Stevensville, Montana, located near the original mission lies at 46° 30′ N., 114° 6′ W. Goode, *World Atlas,* p. 243.

sive. From November 15, 1842, until February 20, of the following year, the temperature was almost constantly 24° below zero on Ramur's [20] [sic] thermometer, and at various times through March during the winter of 1846 it was 27° below zero.

The place now called Saint Mary's was once called *Lkaetlemelsch* or *wooded place* by the Flatheads, while among the Canadians it was referred to as *racine amere*,[21] because of the great quantities of those bitter roots which form a large part of the diet of these people.[22] (See letter to N.P.G. September 1847.)[23]

[20] On the Reaumur scale the melting point of ice is measured as 0°R and the boiling point of water is 80°R. *Encyclopedia Britannica* (24 vols.; Chicago, 1966), XIX, p. 18.

[21] Racine Amere is the French name for the plant, *lewisia rediviva,* commonly referred to as the bitterroot plant.

[22] The Flathead could depend upon a variety of wildlife to supplement the buffalo diet. Flathead Lake provided fish and is consequently the habitat for such fish-eating birds as ospreys, loons and gulls. Native game birds in the area include grouse, ducks and geese. In addition to the usual small game animals, numerous white-tail deer frequent the lake, and in the mountains beyond are elk, moose, Rocky Mountain goats, bighorn sheep and both black and grizzly bears. At some time past buffalo were to be found in the region. Predators include coyotes, weasels, martens, foxes, wildcats, mountain lions, and an occasional lynx and timber wolf. Malouf, *Land Use,* pp. 24-25.

In times of famine the Flatheads even ate the pellicle found between the bark and the wood of certain trees. Finally, of substantial economic importance to the Flathead were the camas and bitterroot plants. These had a profound effect on Flathead military relations. The camas *(quamasta quamash),* and the bitterroot *(lewisia rediviva),* are not found on the semi-arid plains, and the Plains type Indians, lacking adequate vegetable food, sought treaties with the Salish monopolists, enabling them to enter the valleys and gather the plants. In exchange for this privilege, the Plains people were to permit the Salish to enter the eastern grasslands in search of bison. Harry Turney-High, "Cooking Camas and Bitter Root," *Scientific Monthly,* XXXVI (Mar. 1933), p. 265.

[23] This was a reference to Mengarini's annual report to Father John Roothaan, the Very Reverend General of the Society of Jesus in Rome. Davis, *History of St. Ignatius,* p. 2.

8

A Disappearing Tribe

The population of the Flatheads numbers little more than five hundred souls particularly after the losses of this past year 1847, in which eighty-six persons died – the largest number from an epidemic of smallpox.[1] But it was not always so.

About seventy years ago, according to the calculations of the elders, the Flatheads included at least eight hundred families or about four thousand people.[2] Now it

---

[1] Chittenden likens Indian losses in combat to a bagatelle, when measured against death from pandemic disease introduced by the whites. He points especially to the smallpox scourge of 1837 (it had first appeared in 1800). It was introduced by the steamboat *St. Peter,* arriving at Fort Union on June 24, 1837. By the end of the year all the tribes of the Missouri Valley above the Sioux had been stricken. The total mortality among the Blackfeet, Crows, Mandans, Minnetaries and Aricaras was near to 15,000. Hiram Chittenden, *The American Fur Trade of the Far West,* II, pp. 612-19.

Other authorities agree, noting that before the smallpox epidemic of 1781-1782, the number of Indians in the Northwest was between 75,000 and 100,000. After the fever and ague of 1830-31 only fifteen or twenty thousand remained.

[2] Probably eighty per cent of native peoples of the Pacific Northwest were swept away by white man's diseases during the half century that preceded Oregon Trail migration. The first of these white man's plagues was smallpox, which in 1781-1782 swept from the Upper Missouri River to the Pacific Ocean. The second great scourge was "fever and ague," which ravaged the Indian races in 1830-1831. These epidemics spent their fury in short periods of time, but their end did not palliate the later mortality resulting from tuberculosis, measles, sex diseases and liquor.

In response to this destructive onslaught, Father Anthony Ravalli brought

occurred that while a small number had left for a
buffalo hunt, all those remaining in camp were attacked
by a devastating plague which in a very few days killed
everyone with the exception of fifteen children who
were not infected by the disease. Among this number
were Peter the great leader, and old Simon who died
shortly after the arrival of the missionaries and of
whom we have spoken in preceding pages, as well as
others who still live. The disease caused the growth of
large red and black pustules over the entire body, particularly on the chest. Those developing red pustules
died within a few days, but those who were plagued by
the black pustules died almost instantly.[3] During this
same period the epidemic destroyed another entire nation of savages who spoke a different tongue and dwelt
about five days' journey from the Flatheads.[4] Of them
there remained not even the name.

Ten years before this catastrophe visited them it was

---

a vaccine for smallpox from Italy in 1845. When his supply of drugs was
exhausted, he attempted to standardize the herbs which the Indians used. But
he could not convince himself that many of them were of value. He made
alcohol from camas root for use in his drug room. "Only Two of the Original
Buildings Still Standing," *The Montana Standard* (Helena), June 21, 1941,
Section 2, p. 1.

[3] According to Dr. Michael Kogen, Director of Epidemic Disease Study at
USC-County Medical Center, Mengarini's description suggests either regular
or hemoragic smallpox, the latter causing black rather than red lesions. Yet
he questioned the rate of infection and attack, since no epidemic disease has
a nearly total attack; in some instances, it infects at merely the immuniz-
ing level. It is also difficult to understand that the fifteen to survive would
be children, normally the most vulnerable. Michael Kogen, M.D., to Gloria
Lothrop, Los Angeles, June 6, 1968, Per. Corr.

[4] It is difficult to identify this particular tribe since the fever which attacked
in the 1830s, destroyed many entire tribes. As Hall Jackson Kelley wrote in
his "Memoir," by 1834 the Indian population along the Columbia River, which
Lewis and Clark had estimated as being about eight thousand twenty-eight
years before, numbered only four hundred.

presaged by another calamity. The Flatheads were busily collecting roots when they were surprised by a very thick fog which developed into the finest rain of white droplets as dry and bitter as nitrate salts. This was followed by an earthquake similar to the eruption of a volcano.[5] All ceased as a large number of Flatheads who had been instantly killed began to fall here and there. We have never been able to understand from whence this emanated, especially since there is not a vestige of a volcano in all these lands with exception of a place the Canadians call *la loge aux chevreux,* which is a small mountain no more than thirty feet high isolated in the middle of a great plain. At its summit there are eight small pools of spring water, some of which are very cold, others are lukewarm, and others half boiling, and all the terrain nearby is covered with soda.[6] But aside from the fact that this place is at least one hundred miles from the spot where the Flatheads were then located, the most elderly are sure they have always seen this small, possibly volcanic mountain in the same state in which it is presently found.

[5] A possible explanation for the unusual events could have been an intense concentration of sulphur dioxide or sulphur fumes. Such could have produced results somewhat along these lines, although instantaneous death would not have occurred. Robert A. Dightman to Gloria R. Lothrop, Helena, Mont., June 6, 1968, Per. Corr. Recent research indicates that Mt. St. Helens was still active in the early 1800s and probably Mt. Rainier was as well. Richard Dougherty to Gloria R. Lothrop, Pullman, Wash., Nov. 29, 1968. *Ibid.* For historical evidence of these two events see Clifford M. Drury, *Elkanah and Mary Walker;* Kenneth L. Holmes, "Mount St. Helens' Recent Eruptions," *Oreg. Hist. Quar.,* LVI (Sept. 1955), pp. 197-210.

[6] It is possible that the reference is to one of the highest peaks in the western range of the Bearpaw Mountains. Stout, *History of Montana,* I, 94. The reference may also be to a fur rendezvous area known as Prairie de Chevaux. Alexander Ross, *Fur Hunters of the Far West* (Norman, Okla., 1956), I, p. 217.

Moreover, we are convinced that the savages in this region will continue to decrease ever more if it holds true that where whites have penetrated and multiply, the savages diminish and disappear. Undoubtedly, of the many tribes which formerly occupied the entire territory of the United States, now only the name remains (with the exception of a few *Sciavanon* and *Delawares*).[7] The town of Willamette, in fact all of Oregon, offers a forceful example. It is but a few years since the Americans entered the Willamette valley. But from their initial entry to the present, the savages have contracted epidemic diseases each year, and since each epidemic, however slight, is mortal to them, they die by the hundreds each year.

Last year's wagon train was infected with smallpox. Upon arrival at Fort Hall all those who were there were affected and as a result, those who came to Saint Mary's communicated it to all the Flatheads.[8] Those continuing on their journey, infected all the savages

---

[7] The Delawares were recruited into fur trade service which explains their presence in the Interior Columbia Basin. See LeRoy R. Hafen, *Mountain Men*, II, p. 249, note 7.

[8] Statistics give added credence to this report. Observations by Samuel Parker from 1835 to 1837 place the Flathead population at 800. Parker, *Journal*, p. 311. Three years later De Smet rendered a similar opinion as to the number. De Smet, *Voyages aux Montagnes Rocheuses*, p. 331. One might conclude that population factors were fairly constant. But between 1853-1855, Mullan placed the Flathead population at four hundred. It is, therefore, reasonable to conclude that disease of epidemic proportions could have reduced the population by one-half. Merriam provides additional demographic information to support this position. Merriam, *Ethnomusicology of the Flathead Indians*, p. 347.

The decline is made more dramatic by Teit's assertion that the total population of the Flathead tribes sometime after the introduction of the horse around 1725, or at least before the beginning of armed conflict with the Blackfeet, may have been in the neighborhood of 15,000. "Salishan Tribes," p. 314.

they met. As a result the Pend d'Oreilles, the Nez
Perce, the *Caldaj,* the Walla Walla, the Kaius, the
Saluspen, and the Chinook were each attacked by smallpox and a great number died; and at almost the same
time and for the same reason the Blackfeet, the Mandans, the Crows, and the Crees on the other side of the
mountain died in great numbers.[9]

---

[9] Mengarini is not alone in accusing the white man of being the cause of
these mass epidemics. Gibbs concurs that of the diseases to which the Indians
are most subject, venereal in its different forms and smallpox, are assumed to
have been introduced by whites. Gibbs, "Tribes of Western Washington and
Northwestern Oregon," *Cont. to N. Am. Ethn.,* ed. Powell, pp. 227-368.

9

Flathead Life

The Flatheads are of a very serious, analytical and resolute character. They always speak slowly in a low voice. Never do we see one, regardless of how personally agitated or afflicted he may be, betray any external sign, for the Flathead considers anger and melancholy most ill-bred behavior.

When, however, they have decided upon a course of action, whether it be good or bad, it is most difficult to dissuade them unless it be a true friend, particularly a companion from adolescence. Such a Maecenas or patron has absolute power over the soul of a friend. He is refused nothing, and he is able to obtain that which neither the leaders nor the missionary would have been able to. By the same token, neither the missionaries nor the leaders can restrain from a misguided path one who is persuaded by an evil friend who does not wish it. Finally, the Flatheads place so great a store upon the friendship of another that in order to secure it they often give a comrade the shirts from their backs even without being asked.

Like any other tribe, the Flatheads have their tribal and martial music. By it they are recognized and distinguished from other tribes when all gather in reunion. It also inspires in them an incredible courage when battling their enemies. This music is without words. It expresses with simple vowels of *i,a,e*. Furthermore, it is without formal metric structure, being instead composed of a series of chromes.[1] Each note is given an equal emphasis, all of this to the accompaniment of the drum.[2] Because it would be desirable to have some idea of the music, several examples have been added.

Flatheads and Pend d'Oreilles:

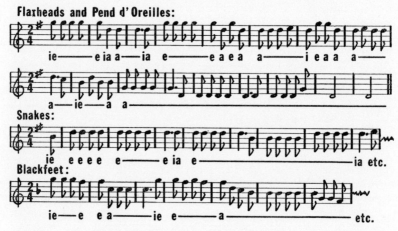

But the Flatheads much prefer the music of the whites, though they possess no talent for vocal music.[3]

---

[1] While no musicological analysis has as yet been completed, some tentative conclusions may be advanced concerning the general character of Flathead music. For additional discussion see Merriam, *Ethnomusicology of the Flathead Indians,* p. 41.

[2] Mengarini's description suggests that the music of the Flatheads was moderately fast and composed of notes having equal value, the chrome by this date having acquired the value of a quarter note. Typical of Indian music, the variations were provided by the free rhythmic structure in which verbal accentuation provides the meter. Mary Ann Bonino to Gloria R. Lothrop, Los Angeles, Sept. 16, 1969, Per. Corr.

[3] The vocal quality employed by singers among the Flatheads is fairly typical of American Indian voice production generally. Using a tight, though

Notwithstanding this, they become so enthusiastic after mastering some new little religious hymn that they repeatedly sing it distorting it in such a manner that it is unrecognizable as they sing it at the top of their voices at least ten times a day.

Both the young people and the small children have an admirable facility and quickness for learning whatever they are taught.[4] This forces one to conclude that if they did not have at least nine months vacation each year, they would be well trained in the arts.

Now let us briefly discuss Flathead government. We do not know exactly how to define it; it is a monarchy, it is anarchy; that is, call it what you want. It could be defined as an anarchic monarchy.[5] Although the Flatheads have always recognized a great leader or king and several other second rank leaders, the only func-

---

open throat, but without employing the full resonance possibilities of the upper nasal cavities, a penetrating quality is produced in the style often labeled as the "clenched-teeth" or "ventriloquistic" style, although it is impossible to determine whether Flatheads used a more dynamic style of vocal production in previous times. Merriam, "Music of the Flathead Indians," p. 20.

Flathead singers sometimes perform alone, but prefer singing with a leader and chorus designated by common consent. The singing today is frequently accompanied by a flageolot, an end blown instrument made from hollowed elderberry wood. *Ibid.,* p. 105.

[4] Turney-High corroborates this ability to learn among Flathead youths, but attributes this to the parents' positive urging that they be helpful. As one informant explained, "We were proudest when we could surprise them with something extra we had done." *Flathead Indians of Montana,* p. 76.

[5] George Gibbs has made similar observations regarding the tribal polity of the Northwest Indians. He notes the absence of clan divisions within the tribe, the absence of emblematic distinctions resembling totem and the limited power of the nominal chief. *Cont. to Indian Ethn.,* pp. 184-85. The reason for this anarchic state may have resulted from incomplete assimilation. Tribal organization as opposed to the informal organization of village life was not native to the Indians of the Interior Plateau. It was a Plains trait superimposed once contact between the two cultures was made possible by the advent of the horse during the first quarter of the eighteenth century. Ray, *Cultural Relations,* p. 14.

tions of the first consisted of marching at the head of
the rest when hunting and of making some inspirational
observations to the others each morning and evening.
The secondary leaders have no authority except in
name, save for those who have been called heads because several families follow them.[6] As for the rest,
there is no one law, no one ordinance, and consequently,
no subordination among the citizens. There is no one
punishment, instead each person is absolute master over
himself; to do whatever he wants, going wherever he
pleases, and treating others according to the impulse of
his passions without fearing revenge from those he has
offended.

But nevertheless, in years past the Flatheads had
some kind of great leader not only in name, but one who
also forced submission whenever he was not obeyed.
The oldest members of the tribe can still recount many
of the details.

As a result of the instructions provided by the Iroquois, the Flatheads learned to distinguish more clearly
between good and evil.[7] The leaders began to persuade
them and to punish the more guilty with blows as
stinging as those used to whip a horse.[8] This punish-

---

6 The many functionaries besides the hereditary head chief were each given
the title *Imigum*. Hubert H. Bancroft, *Native Races* (5 vols.; San Francisco,
1882), III, p. 155.

7 Elliott advances a unique counter-argument against the Iroquois influence. He notes the much earlier arrival of the Bible-carrying mountain man,
Jedediah Smith. It is suggested that it was he who planted the seeds for the
future Flathead delegation. Elliott, "Religion Among the Flatheads," pp. 1-8.

8 Some researchers claim that flogging appeared around 1700. For almost
two hundred years one of the most important symbols of chieftainship was
the whip, a long lash made of buckskin loaded with buckshot. Informants say
that one hundred lashes with the loaded whip laid on by a muscular chief
was as severe as the judicial execution and exile which it replaced. Turney-
High, *Flathead Indians of Montana*, p. 47.

ment resulted from conviction rather than authority. It became so firmly entrenched and was so widely respected among the Flatheads that they not only allowed themselves to be punished by their leaders, but they would often request to be flogged, convinced that only in that way could they regain their reputations. After the arrival of the missionary, the guilty easily made the transition from these punishments to the penances imposed in confession.[9]

From the beginning the missionaries directed all their efforts toward encouraging submission to the tribal leaders, making clear to the latter their obligation to watch over the conduct of their citizens, and expounding upon the power of these chiefs before the citizens. But despite all their efforts, only in recent times have they been capable to obtain some slight results, but it really is on the one hand the native indolence of the savage which forces the chiefs to almost constant inaction. On the other hand, the obstinacy of the citizens trained since childhood to do always as they please does not favorably dispose them toward the simplest admonitions.

From this state of affairs rise many grave consequences which in themselves would be enough to destroy a missionary's morale. The leaders themselves complain that the citizens do not listen to them, but they will not believe that they themselves are the reason. If asked how they behaved in the past, the chiefs who consider themselves strong answer that on occasion they themselves would go with club or gun in hand in order to enforce obedience. But if we reply, "Why do you not

---

[9] For a fuller discussion of the "gastigo," see Palladino, *Indian and White in the Northwest*, p. 100; O'Connor, "Records of the Flatheads," p. 105.

do the same now," the only response is a profound silence and a raised eyebrow. Who is it who blinds them?

In addition to the apathy already referred to there is a tendency toward faulty judgment which until now has been impossible to destroy notwithstanding the many oft repeated instructions on this subject. Besides, a chief who is honest and who may wish to please will not make a move in matters affecting another individual, will not utter a word implying the slightest criticism if it causes another pain. And why? In order to avoid feeling ill at ease, and in order that the other party have no cause to complain of injury. Therefore, every specific criticism, even one made by a father of his son, is considered evil speech.[10]

The Flatheads confuse crudely zealous behavior with violence. For example, if a woman has forcefully rejected a man tempting her to evil action, she will immediately rush crying and sobbing to the missionary to accuse herself of having spoken harshly when alarmed. And we are not without those women who will go to chiefs for a flogging in order to lessen the guilt they feel.

Now, excluding their official roles, the conduct of the Flathead chiefs is reprehensible. They do not even place themselves in a position to be perturbed, being satisfied with giving orders and exhorting in vague

[10] This consideration toward others is still evident within the culture. Flatheads are very careful to add "please" to any request, and carefully make the distinction between "you" and "thou" contained in the Salishan grammar. In fact, the intimate "you" is rarely used. Because of this reticence to offend, Flathead social control rests primarily upon ridicule. "The mirrored self to the Flathead is the most important self." Turney-High, *Flathead Indians of Montana,* p. 44. See Rappagliosi, *Memorie,* pp. 105-06.

words and generalities. Even if the orders were not followed and consequently the entire tribe suffered, they would see themselves as having done too much, even uttering: *"Tasgest,* it is not good." One such inept procedure greatly hinders the growth of the mission and it has forced the missionaries to urge the great chiefs to appoint new leaders who are more adept in controlling the citizens.[11]

As a result, the actual government of the Flatheads has been structured as follows: a great leader or king; a prefect or master of the camp who is immediately responsible for the government of the citizens. All of these have a substitute or adjutant. Six of the eldest tribesmen serve as counselors to the first three, and twenty brave young warriors, selected from the best in the tribe are always prepared to follow the orders of the master of the camp or in his absence his substitute.

---

[11] Mengarini speaks feelingly on the weakness of governmental leadership as a result of his own experiences of the year before. The selection from his letter included as Appendix B, emphasizes the ineffectiveness of the chiefs and the council in combatting the schism perpetrated by Little Faro in 1847.

10

Challenges Facing the Missionary

Certainly many would be deceived into thinking that once the first difficulty had been surmounted, all else solves itself in the savage mission. Instead the development of such missions, and especially those of the Flatheads, encounters many obstacles. What we have described of their government is but one and by no means the greatest. Many others, one more difficult than the next, are still to be surmounted.

The hunt, for example, is one. It alone causes an indescribable amount of damage and waste. It is not an exaggeration, but rather from the experience of many years that I claim that this single factor is enough to render completely useless and without fruit all the efforts of a missionary to train their souls and to civilize them. First of all, the nomadic, vagabond life which they are forced to pursue as in times past, adhering to those ancient ideas, causes them to remain in their savage state. Furthermore, the passions which slumbered while they dwelt in villages are reawakened even more strongly during the hunt. Occasions of sin are not lacking, for the devil does not sleep. It is certain that in a single summer hunt more sins are committed than during three full years of village life. In addition, all the traditional teachings and whatever else they have learned are completely forgotten. Whether a missionary accompanies them or not, it is impossible for them to receive new instructions. The leaders, even if they attempted to, cannot at all oversee their subjects during this time.[1] Consequently, upon the savages' return, the missionary discovers numerous spiritual scars, many of them incurable, incurred during the hunting season. In disappointment he is forced to begin everything all over again as if it were the first day of instruction.[2] To understand how this occurs, it is best to know how the hunt is conducted.

Since wild life becomes more rare each year, the Flatheads are forced to break up into bands in order to search them out. With particular frequency these bands are joined by savages of other nations for mutual protection, including the Pend d'Oreilles, Nez Perce, Spokan, etc. But let us exclude those who have not

---

[1] When writing of the buffalo hunt Father Michael Accolti observed: "They [the Flatheads] spend at least half the year at the hunt in pursuit of buffalo. During this time they have none of the ministrations which could be offered to them by an accompanying priest." Accolti to Roothaan, Santa Clara, Calif., Feb. 28, 1850, Jes. Arch., Gonzaga Univ.

[2] Father Point focuses upon an entirely different reaction to the temptations of the hunt. He writes of the Flathead: "More mistrustful of themselves than ever as they left for their hunt, they felt a need for adding three new invocations to their pious practices. The invocations were, 'St. Michael, pray for us; St. Raphael, pray for us; St. Hubert, pray for us.' These three were chosen because they had learned that St. Michael was the protector of the brave; St. Raphael, the guide of travelers; and St. Hubert, the patron of hunters." *Wilderness Kingdom*, p. 181.

Point goes on to liken the summer hunt to a pious pilgrimage during which the chiefs and the elite of the braves led the way to the communion rail. He concludes by observing that by the end of the hunt only one old woman had failed to go to Confession. *Ibid.*, p. 47; Point, "Recollections of the Rocky Mountain Missions," pp. 298-321.

received the missionary's instruction. Let us instead speak of those who have. The Flatheads, once on the trail, are always out of their tents before sunrise.[3] They untether the horses which have been hobbled during the night, and as a precaution against enemies they follow the horses to pasture with rifle in hand.[4] There they remain until the women have broken camp and have prepared for departure. While the women load the horses, the men still unfed, with rifles in hand, mount their horses and disappear.[5] Dispersing in groups of three, or five, or ten together, they ride at some distance from each other until they reach the summit in pursuit of a deer or roe-buck and also in watchful anticipation of the enemy as they continue their search for buffalo.[6] Returning to camp after nightfall, the members of the company eat a piece of raw or cooked meat, if they

---

[3] For purposes of mutual protection the lodges were pitched as close together as possible, the position of the tent in the circle being assigned by the sub-chief. Pitching the lodges was a task easily accomplished by a woman in fifteen minutes. Vernon D. Malan, "Language and Social Change Among the Flathead Indians" (Unpublished Master's Thesis, Mont. St. Univ., 1948), p. 46.

[4] Only the band's herd, or secondary horses, were kept in a fenced camp ring. Each man's prized hunting horse, or the primary horses, were tethered by a foreleg in front of the owner's tent. Because of their economic importance, each day before all else, the owner would patiently guard him for an hour as he grazed, before returning to breakfast. Linked to the horse complex were the number of bison robes a family possessed. It took horses to acquire and to transport a large number. Turney-High, *Flathead Indians of Montana,* p. 132.

[5] The morning meal generally consisted of dried meat, camas, bitterroot, and berries. If fresh meat was available, some of it might be boiled or roasted. A portion of food was placed either on leaves or grass or in a large pine knot bowl. Their long hair served as a towel for wiping their hands after eating. Thwaites, *Early Western Travels,* XXVII, p. 300.

[6] During the hunt the Salish aimed his arrow at the back of the bison's shoulder in hope of its piercing his heart. If, however, this was impossible, the kidney was pierced, despite the consequent tendency to embitter the meat. Malan, "Language and Social Change Among the Flathead," p. 39.

have bagged some game. If not, they relieve their hunger with some roots and fall asleep in order to pursue the same maneuver on the morrow.

While the braves are thus dispersed upon the mountainsides, the rest of the camp, mostly composed of women and children and an occasional elderly chief, establish another camp ground. As soon as the horses are unloaded, the women begin to cut wood for the fires as well as for the construction of horse corrals, so that when the missionary issues the call to prayer, he is greeted by none save some old women and children.[7] The men and above all the young braves, who are, as a matter of fact, those in most need of instruction, are either guarding the horses or still scattered upon the mountainside. It is no better when they have killed a buffalo or when they are in camp; the guarding of the horses never ceases.[8] Consequently, amidst the labor of the savages with whom he finds himself, the missionary is superfluous, save as a witness to all the misery that befalls them without in any way being able to relieve it.

For example, the youths who were reasonably tractable in the villages, during the hunt become as obstinate and hardheaded as the buffalo. Often when they dis-

[7] The old people worked busily around the camp at such tasks as they were capable of performing. The men would braid bison-hair ropes or make drinking horns and stone pounders or toys for the children, while the women looked after the children or assisted in smoking the meat. *Ibid.,* p. 60.

[8] The Flatheads had comparatively large herds of horses which were notably superior to most Indian cayuses. Using flint knives, they castrated their horses, realizing that, if gelded after maturity, the horse retained more of the vigor of a stallion. As a result, one Blackfoot brave confided to Governor Isaac Stevens that he "stole" the first Flathead horse he came across for it was sure to be a good one. This reputation brought traders from as far away as Salt Lake City to procure horses for the Pony Express. Woody, *Cont. to the Hist. Soc. of Mont.* (2 vols.; Helena, Mont., 1896), I, p. 148.

cover a herd of buffalo, instead of informing their leaders, according to custom and strict rule, they attack the herd, shouting like wolves in their enthusiasm, killing several and causing the rest to flee thirty or forty miles away. Thus they force the entire camp to go hungry. If they learn that another nation is encamped nearby, they hurry there, and one will return with one woman, who will remain there during the rest of the hunt, and God knows the rest.[9] Without enumerating all of the temporal sins which the hunt occasions, be assured that in addition to those described, the savages commit all the rest.

While on the hunt, some fall from their horses and die. Others remain crippled the rest of their lives. Others drink putrified, stagnant water and succumb to infection. Others are blinded by the snow and dust.

What can be added then of the encounter of the Flatheads with their enemies?[10] War occurs almost every year, and often more frequently. The number of widows, having lost their young husbands in battle, multiplies in number. Without question, war, far more than the hunt, continues to keep the savages fierce and barbarous, rendering them incapable of fixing their attention upon the faith which they have embraced.

The infestation by Blackfeet presents yet another

---

[9] The acquisition of female captives was almost as honorable as the capture of a horse. It was accompanied by shouting and rejoicing in camp, since her work value was of economic importance to the members of the tribe. Of course, to this could be added her often prized estate as a sexual partner in concubinage to the chief or the foremost braves. Turney-High, *Flathead Indians of Montana*, pp. 130-31.

[10] In fact, the verb generally used for "going to war," literally means "stealing horses." Furthermore, the term "horse-thief" was an honorable one to the Flathead for it signified "warrior." *Ibid.*, p. 62.

serious impediment to the progress of the mission.[11] For
our savages, horses represent wealth and life.[12] Without
them they are unable to procure the necessities of survival, hence their importance.[13] Thus attracted, enemies
will not leave them alone. Each year they successfully
flee with a great quantity of Flathead horses. In order
to lose as few as possible, the Flatheads are forced to
maintain continuous surveillance during all seasons of
the year, and consequently remain in the grazing fields
almost all day. This is not only detrimental to their
spiritual life, but it also makes them physically ill.
Many die of consumption induced by the cold. Nevertheless, this care is often ineffective, because in the dark
of night the enemy stealthily enters the village, cuts the
ropes holding the horses, mounts them and escapes.[14]

11 During the latter part of the eighteenth century the Blackfeet moved
south and west from Canada, acquiring guns but not horses along the way.
Once on the Plains, the Blackfeet ignored reciprocal economic treaties made
with the Piegan for the Flathead to hunt through their territory in exchange
for the right to gather vegetable food lacking on the Plains. Lax organization
among the Algonkian provided no authority for enforcing such "international"
agreements and resulted in repeated violent encounters between Blackfeet and
Flathead. *Ibid.,* p. 116.

12 With the introduction of the horse complex, the wealth concept becomes
an equine concept. Only a man rich in horses could acquire a large supply of
pemmican. Only he could pack it home and trade it for other articles. *Ibid.,*
p. 105.

13 Merriam suggests that the Flathead adopted the horse as a means of
transportation between 1710 and 1735. It was after this that it became cus-
tomary to make one or two trips to the Plains each year to hunt buffalo. On
these trips the Flathead came into contact with Plains people, particularly the
Blackfeet, who became "traditional" enemies. Merriam, *Ethnomusicology of
the Flathead Indians,* p. 124.

14 Those at St. Mary's also commented upon the seriousness of the Blackfoot
problem. Brother Claessens narrated: "The Blackfeet were a great trouble to
us. So much so that at 3 miles from the mission we were not sure of our lives.
Brother Joseph [Specht] and I spent many a weary night in sharp lookout on
the top of our bastions with our guns. Fr. De Smet bade me never to undress
at night, and to make a wooden cannon to keep the Blackfeet away." Claessens to [?], n.d., cited in Bischoff, *Jesuits in Old Oregon,* p. 67.

From what we have outlined arises the cause of another great obstacle to our spiritual instruction. Those who guard the horses during the day are in fact the youths who would be the hope of the missionary since they are more easily trained and more responsive to instruction. A missionary who today may be catechizing fifty families, tomorrow may have only ten among whom he may find only one or two of the fifty he instructed before.

Without a doubt, all these difficulties are serious and will not cease until the Flatheads will have the wherewithal to live and clothe themselves within their villages. Otherwise it seems assured that a mission established amidst a people increasingly compelled to withdraw, will find itself as it was in the beginning, even if it lasts a hundred years.

Even the Flatheads who possess no great wisdom understand this fact, and for some time have had the greatest desire to stop leading a life which could be called a continuing death. There have been many who without outside urging have disposed of their horses and their peltries in order to purchase a cow or two from the white men and build themselves a wooden house. Alone they have begun to till their little farms. Yet this itself places them in the arms of extremity, because on the one hand, one or two cows and a small farm are not sufficient to feed and clothe an entire family.[15] On the other hand they cannot abandon their animals. In any case it is best to leave in order to avoid

---

[15] Nevertheless, Gibbs at another point observed that some of the first herds of cattle in Montana were possessed by Flathead. They procured most of them from men who traded for worn-out stock along the Oregon Trail late in the 1840s and who wintered the animals in the relative safety of Flathead Country. Gibbs, *Report of Explorations*, I, p. 323.

starvation. But they cannot leave for they have sold their horses. Placed in this incredibly discouraging position, what should they do? Sell their cow; abandon their small farm? Will they again throw themselves into farming, or will they withdraw ever more into the forests, rarely being seen and always becoming more savage?

The indifference of the parents toward the education of their children is yet another obstacle.[16] If the missionary could at least have the youths within earshot, if not near him, he would perhaps achieve something by guiding them. But this is in fact impossible. Consequently, the children grow up with the same habits, defects and vices as their parents. Fortunate indeed is that child possessing a mother and father who are wholly committed to their faith and who have entirely renounced their ancient traditions, and in all ways follow the instruction of the missionary. Such circumstances are but rare.

As soon as a boy reaches five or six years of age, he leaves his tent with bow and arrow in hand each morning after having prayed and having eaten. In the company of other youngsters he ventures into the meadow, not returning until dusk when neither mother nor father will ask him where he went, nor with whom, nor what he did.[17] When a son reaches fourteen, his parents

---

[16] Other researchers agree that the Flathead did not take the prepubertal education of his offspring seriously, although he was bound to provide for his offspring's training in the tribal mores. But with adolescence both boys and girls were given serious training for adult responsibility. Turney-High, *Flathead Indians of Montana*, pp. 76-81.

[17] The fact that children were allowed to roam in the forest can be explained by the fact that the adults in the culture began early to inculcate the concept of the "guardian spirit" into the young boys and, to a lesser extent,

are completely unable to command him. Their only recourse is to entreat him. If he refuses, as ordinarily happens, the mother and father are forced to satisfy their own entreaty. This in turn encourages an increasing arrogance and insurmountable obstinacy in their children.

Now let us assume that the missionary performs his duty, firmly instructing the parents as well as the children, punishing this one or that one by depriving him of Holy Communion, which for the savages is the greatest punishment. The missionary will achieve something as long as they remain in the village, but once having left, the one will cease his watchfulness, the other his obedience. Upon their return the missionary is forced to begin anew with the same instruction and the same penances. And when the parents decide to condemn the already excessive insolence of their children, the youths having grown older, rebel against their parents and mounting their horse simply move two or three hundred miles away.

Another obstacle is presented by the women.[18] From the beginning we encountered two most unseemly traits among the Flatheads. One was that men cruelly mistreated their wives, beating them and trampling them beneath their feet, often causing the death of children yet unborn. The other problem was that some women were such masters over their men, that the latter were not allowed to manage even the smallest household

the girls. When they were still very young, the children were sent by their fathers on unimportant missions purely for the sake of training the children by forcing them to find their way around in the forests. Forbis, "Religious Acculturation of the Flathead Indians," p. 21.

[18] See Chap. IV, note 9, herein.

detail or manner of living. At morning and evening the wife served portions of food to both husband and children. This not infrequently aroused the ire of the husband, for if his wife was displeased with him, he was certain to pass the day without eating, or at best to receive a few animal entrails as would befit a dog.

The missionaries pressed their attack against these abuses. The men being more reasonable surrendered easily, and completely abandoned their barbarous treatment, so that we never again heard of abortions caused by their maltreatment. But since the Flathead women possess most difficult and inconstant natures, we were unable to achieve but the slightest consideration regarding their husbands. The ancient custom of female despotism consequently still exists in its entirety.[19]

The men do nothing but slay the animals. These, once killed, immediately pass into the control of the women who dispose as they wish of both the meat and the fur. Since not only the clothes they wear but almost everything else, including the tent, the saddles, the sacks, cords, etc., belong to the women, it is useless to ask a man if he has supplies or skins. He will answer that he

---

[19] Father Joset makes a similar assertion regarding the Indians along the Columbia adding that it is not unusual to see a woman step before the council and upbraid the chief. The woman's position was secured by her economic position. The fish delivered to her for processing, the fruits and berries she gathered, even the rushes she manufactured into mats to build her lodge, were items to be traded for provisions and even horses. The house and its contents were, therefore, considered hers, and the husband was dependent upon her for his sustenance. Joseph Joset, s.j., "Chronology of the Rocky Mountain Indians," Joset Papers, Box xxxiv, Jes. Arch., Gonzaga Univ. Other evidence negates this assertion. To the contrary, other accounts portray the Flathead woman as a paragon of industrious docility. Point, *Wilderness Kingdom,* p. 150. Also refer to Chapter I of the "Memorie" where Mengarini notes the desirability of Flathead wives among white trappers.

knows nothing about it. It is best to question his wife.[20] There are a number of women who own a wooden house, a cow or two, and perhaps are owners of something else as well.[21]

Among the greatest difficulties encountered in developing this mission is the presence of white men, even white Catholics, who in the estimation of the savages are incomparably courageous.[22] Because it was covetous desire which led these white Catholics to the lands of the Flatheads, it is almost impossible to find among them any who are loyal in the practice of their faith. Thus the savage is constantly exposed to moral scandal. They have, consequently, learned to swear in French, in English, and to cheat in the others.

Despite the Flatheads' traditional habits and the other grave difficulties which have rendered the mission

---

[20] In explanation of the wife's economic supremacy it should be noted that after the introduction of the horse Flathead women were included in the hunt in order to dress and preserve the buffalo meat which could then be stored in greater quantities. Gunther, "Westward Movement of Some Plains Traits," *American Anthropologist*, LII (Apr.-June 1950), pp. 174-80.

From the moment the hunter deposited the game with his wife, it was legally hers, and all therefrom as well. For example, from the skins she made the covers for the tents which in theory she owned. Turney-High, *Flathead Indians of Montana*, pp. 91, 100.

[21] Some have further ascribed this female dominance to the increasingly diminished number of men as a result of warfare – a point made by Mengarini. Others have added to the obvious economic advantage women presented, the fact that the Salishan culture was basically matrilineal.

On the other hand, recent research by Ray has indicated no such matriarchal structure. This would be predictable in terms of the cultural characteristics of unspecialized hunters and gatherers as indeed the Flatheads were. To prove his point, Ray adds that even today the Flathead hunter's wife strictly avoids the rear of the lodge where the meat is first brought in. Ray, *Culture Elements*, p. 127.

[22] The corrupting influence of the whites is also warned against by De Smet, as recorded in Thwaites, *Early Western Travels*, XXVII, p. 296.

at Saint Mary's a difficult one, we cannot deny that with all these efforts we have still scored a few victories, and the devil has witnessed some great defeats.

Of the medicine known as magic we no longer even speak.[23] The hand game which often ruined entire families has been entirely abandoned for five years at least.[24] Nevertheless, during the hunt there are continuing occasions of sin and during these times when they are reunited with other tribes, the savages have bad example continually displayed before their eyes. Polygamy has not existed for years. Of the many shameful

[23] One might question the accuracy of Mengarini's observation in light of the problems others have encountered in discussing the Flathead magic. As Turney-High says: "A conscientious ethnographer cannot get a compendium of trustworthy *sumesh* dreams. Only the completely acculturized or untrustworthy will discuss the matter. Sumesh was, and among honest Indians still is, strictly a matter of personal property. . . No Flathead who sincerely thinks he has *sumesh* is going to give this to an ethnographer except under circumstances of extraordinary friendship or filial relation. To ask a Flathead to describe his medicine experience is considered an unforgiveable impertinence. Therefore, although the writer has heard several alleged *sumesh* songs and has been told of some purported medicine experiences, he considers them utterly unreliable." *Flathead Indians of Montana,* p. 28.

Such silence might suggest a certain hesitation on the part of the Flatheads to share their secret customs with the priests. Withall, De Smet interpreted the change more optimistically: "Not a vestige of their former superstitions can be discovered. Their confidence in us is unlimited. They believe without any difficulty the most profound mysteries of our holy religion, as soon as they are proposed to them, and they do not even suspect that we might be deceived, or even could wish to decieve them. Thwaites, *Early Western Travels,* XXVII, p. 288.

[24] George Gibbs provides a description of the handgame or *it-lu-kam.* "There are several games, the principle of which is the same. In one, a small piece of bone is passed rapidly from hand to hand, shifted behind the back, etc., and the object of the contending party being to ascertain in which hand it is held. Each side is furnished with five or ten small sticks, which serve to mark the game, one stick being given by the guesser whenever he loses, and received whenever he wins. Gibbs, "Tribes of Western Washington and Northwestern Oregon," p. 206.

sins [committed] during the time they dwelt in the village, we no longer speak.[25] Work has replaced the extreme laziness which existed among the men. And not only do we count skilled workmen among the adults, but children of eight or ten manage an axe very well, providing all the firewood used in the mission.[26]

[25] Apparently, the lessons taught by the Black Robes during the buffalo hunting era were not forgotten. In 1879 an official Indian Agent's report noted that, "All of the Indians on this reservation [Jocko] are brought under the influence of religion and are practical Catholics. *Polygamy is punished as a crime by tribal law,* and the marriage rite, which is in every case performed by missionaries, is respected and enforced." Ronan, *Historical Sketch of the Flathead Indian,* p. 94. (Italics supplied.)

[26] Those young men who had been raised at the mission had been brought up as farmers. Joset observed that they acquired new habits. Most of all they were attached to the house. Joseph Joset, s.j., "Chronology of the Rocky Mountain Missions," Joset Papers, Box xcvi, Jes. Arch., Gonzaga Univ.

11

Faith of the Flatheads

Since the Flatheads are fervently devoted to religion, they place great emphasis upon all related to it. On all occasions they perform the rituals in an excellent manner. The rosary, medals, and the scapular have discouraged a great number of sins. These three items constantly hang on their breasts. Such importance is placed upon them that when they are lost, even grown men cry in sorrow. Reciting prayers and singing is their life.[1] With the exception of those who stand guard in the tents, all the others run to the church at the first peel of the bell each morning and evening. *For the Flatheads each day is Sunday:*[2] this expression was included in an eyewitness account of an Anglican minister, who marveled at the great wealth of our church.[3] The congre-

---

[1] One of the more frequently recited prayers was the Pater Noster. The Flathead version of the Lord's Prayer in Flathead is recorded in De Smet's *Oregon Missions,* p. 409.

[2] Sunday, however, was announced by raising a flag on a pole, called *Schazze'us* in Salishan. As a result of this particular Sunday ritual, the Lord's Day was henceforth referred to as *Schazze'us.* Palladino, "Historical Notes on the Flathead," p. 9.

[3] To this date no trace of any part of the St. Mary's mission plan has been found. The reason may be, as Father Ravalli reported, that after the closing of the mission, several packages of records and documents were lost while the departing missionaries forded a river. Schoenberg, "Memorandum Regarding St. Mary's Existing Log Church," ms., Jes. Arch., Gonzaga Univ.

gation of the Immaculate Heart of Mary, devoted to the conversion of sinners, was established among the Flatheads on Whitsunday last year, 1847, but it was already more than a year that we had been preparing for this event, particularly with our prayers. But our natives do not know what it means to have patience and to do the will of God. As a result they sometimes come to the missionary complaining that it is the same. This one or that one for whom they are praying refuses to be converted.

The order of daily spiritual exercises follows a definite pattern. At sunrise we ring the *Angelus Dei,* half an hour later the bell is rung for Mass.[4] The Flatheads begin with a morning offering recited in their native language, then the Our Father, the Hail Mary, and the Credo; the commandments of God and of the Church, and the four acts of Faith, Hope, Charity, and Contrition. Having finished the prayers, we begin the recitation of the Rosary which is interrupted only briefly shortly before the elevation of the Host and at the Communion, at which time we sing a hymn to Jesus in the Blessed Sacrament. When the Mass is finished, the missionary instructs (except on Saturday which is reserved for confessions). After this we recite the litany of the Blessed Virgin, then an Our Father, a Hail Mary, and an act of contrition for the conversion of sinners, concluding with a hymn of thanksgiving.

During the course of the morning, the missionary visits the sick, giving the medicines according to their

---

[4] The Angelus is a short devotion in honor of the Incarnation, repeated three times each day, morning, noon and evening at the sound of the bell. *The Catholic Encyclopedia,* I, p. 486.

needs. Half an hour before noon the bells are again rung for the *Angelus*. Two hours later it is time for the children's catechism instruction which is opened with singing of the *Ave Maria* and followed by the recitation of the lesson, the questioning and the simplest of explanations. We conclude with a little hymn. One hour before sunset the bells are rung for a second recitation of the prayers offered in the morning.

On Saturdays the bells are rung for confession which is offered on a rotating basis. In other words, the first week the men confess, the second week the women, the third the young people, the fourth the children. As a result each one goes to confession at least once a month. Without this division all would go to confession each week, and even every day if he were allowed. This the missionary cannot permit since it is impossible to hear four hundred confessions each week or each day.[5]

On Sunday, Mass is sung and instructions are given after the Gospel. An act of contrition is recited after the Sanctus, and after singing a hymn during the elevation, the congregation recites a passage from the *Capi*[6] [Acts of the Apostles], followed by the recitation of two other acts in preparation for Holy Communion. The same is done after the *Agnus Dei*. Once the Communion is finished they recite two acts of thanksgiving.

---

[5] Examples of the penances given to the Indians, found among the papers of Father Joseph Joset, are undoubtedly representative. "Patrick – every day one pair of beads as long as he lives; Isabelle – one pair of beads every Saturday for one year and avoid anger; Mary Frances – two pairs of beads every day and every Saturday keep her tongue." "Penance list for Indians," p. 1, Joset Papers, Box 1, Jes. Arch., Gonzaga Univ.

[6] Mengarini's colloquialism is somewhat confusing. This could be a reference to readings from the writings of the Fathers of the Church. On the other hand, it could mean a selected reading from the "Acts of Apostles," as noted.

This they repeat after the Last Gospel. After Mass we conduct the ferial day rituals.[7] That is, after the first Mass, since there is yet another one for those who have remained on guard in their tents.

All return to church to recite the Rosary when the bells are rung about an hour before noon. Two hours after noon the general catechism class is convened, after which evening prayers are offered and the litanies are sung. Together we recite the *Memorare* along with the Hail Mary for the conversion of sinners, then we offer benediction of the Blessed Sacrament. After evening devotions, when time and circumstance permit, we allow the youngsters to compete in games on the green. The victors are given some small rewards.

The patron's day for the village is the Feast of the Immaculate Conception of Mary.[8] On this day as on Christmas and Easter, a shot is fired after each toll of the bell. Before Mass we distribute blessed bread to everyone, and during evening catechism those who have performed most diligently are rewarded. In all of the other ecclesiastical ceremonies the rites of the Church are strictly observed.

In conclusion, it would not be inappropriate to say a little something more about the physical appearance of the mission. Until now the missionaries have lived in

---

[7] *Feria,* the Latin word for "free day," denoted a day upon which the people, especially the slaves, were not obliged to work, and on which there were no court sessions. Today the term *feria* is used to denote days of the week with the exception of Sunday and Saturday. *The Catholic Encyclopedia,* VI, p. 43.

[8] The feast, observed on Dec. 8, is based upon the doctrine declared by Pope Piux IX, promulgating the dogma that the Blessed Virgin Mary "in the first instant of her conception, by a singular privilege and grace granted by God, in view of the merit of Jesus Christ, the Saviour of the human race, was preserved exempt from all stain of original sin." *Ibid.,* VII, pp. 674-81.

a temporary house and church in some animal skin tents belonging to the Flatheads. But we have begun to build a finer, more spacious church, a house for the mission-aries, and a permanent village for the savages. Since enemy harassment does not allow the construction of homes in separate locations, the village is being built in the quadrangular shape of a fortress. Each house is fifty feet away from the next. Each is about twenty square feet in size and twelve feet high. Around it is a lawn of sixty square feet. The outside walls of the village are fifteen feet high and are constructed in such a manner that one wall provides major support for the other, as well as a rampart in case of attack. All the construction is of crude brick. The parks provide the savages with a place to corral their animals. Every day these greens will be cleaned by each family. Until all the village is maintained as well as possible, a Prefect of Sanitation will be appointed to supervise.

Since the houses which form the quadrangle are not sufficient for all the families, the village is divided into four parts, each of which is under the care of a head whose house is nearer the town's center which is marked by a cross. Since the savages are never as happy as when they are in the forest, poplars will be planted within as well as outside the village in order to provide shade in summertime. On the map which follows, the color black indicates the construction not yet begun, and the color red, the construction which has either been initiated or completed.[9]

---

[9] A search to locate this map has proved futile.

Appendices

Appendix A

Mengarini's Original Request for a
Missionary Post

*The following letter written by Mengarini on December 25,
1839, while still a seminarian in Rome, clearly reveals his zealous
religious dedication, enhanced as he notes by Bishop Joseph
Rosati's description of the Flathead delegation's search for Black
Robes. The text is translated and reproduced from a microcopy
of the original manuscript.*

Very Reverend Father
Prov. Rome – Rome
Dec. 25, 1839
F. Schol. Gregory Mengarini

After mature examination and with the approval of my spiritual
director I place at the feet of Your Reverence thru the hands of the
Reverend Father Provincial this my request, that for the greater glory
of God you may deign to answer my supplication. The request I make
of Your Reverence is one which grew with my vocation to the Company of Jesus. In other words about fifteen years ago was born in me
a vocation to the foreign missions which continued to grow. In as
many years there has not been one moment in which I have had contrary inclinations toward one or the other. In fact each day for eleven
years I have implored Saint Francis Xavier to aid me in pursuing what
one might call this second vocation from God.

Does it surprise you, Your Reverence, that in the past I have not
revealed this, my desire, although I was continually drawn to do it,
especially when you sent the circular letters in which you urged us to
heed the call of the missions. I was held back because of the limited

virtue I found in myself, the burden of teaching in which I was involved and the fact that I was not yet ordained. I felt it was not yet the opportune time; therefore I had resigned myself to wait until receiving Holy Orders. This I would have done, had not God, our Master, during the Spiritual Exercises of last October deigned to look with pity upon me, and infuse within me a new spirit, which I deeply cherish and which I hope will only grow stronger with time. Together with many other graces which were unexpected, and undeserved, He placed in my heart such urgings to confess all to Your Reverence, that doing so, I would have countered my conscience.

I am as certain of this desire, as I am of my entry into the Company, therefore, I request the foreign missions of Your Paternity and if you should ask where, I would answer any place, but my heart has been, and always remains there, where the poor souls have no one to help them escape the hands of the devil, and where there is the greatest hope, in fact to give both life and blood for love of Jesus, our Captain.

Let my testimony be the tears of happiness which I shed as I write this, may God in his compassion not render me unworthy because of my sins. When I declared to the spiritual director my resolution to offer myself to Your Reverence, he held me back from doing it for the present, in order to better understand the will of God, and to see in what state of mind I would be in time of desolation. In truth, two days did not pass before God allowed my heart and mind to fill with apprehension of all types of dangers, of hardships the likes of which are encountered in such a ministry, that simply to think of them forced me to tremble, the demon who saw the opportune moment did not remain inert and attempted with a thousand suggestions as much as he could to dissuade me from manifesting this to Your Reverence. If I were to tell you how much illumination I received from God in that time of double temptation I would be forced to go on at length. I will say only that withal, it did not serve but to make me better understand that this was a true vocation from God, and that I would emerge from this more strong and more resolute than before. This, in fact, is what the spiritual director specifically advised me to manifest to Your Reverence. Therefore, as far as hardships and dangers of all sorts, none can be more serious than those that with the help of God I feel I have already been able to conquer.

My Father, I say no more of this. Regarding the particular qualities which Your Reverence outlined in the requirements for the missions in 1833, I could assure verbally or in writing of my competence. Let it be as Your Reverence prefers. In the meantime, permit me upon the conclusion of my supplication to again beseech and implore Your Reverence in the name of the passion and death of our Divine Captain, Jesus Christ, and of His most precious blood which He shed for many poor souls who are irreparably lost because they have no one to guide them; that you grant me this favor, and do not close that door that our servant the Apostle St. Francis Xavier opened at such a dear price for those, especially of this Company. If Your Reverence believes that I am still too unworthy, at least, My Father, pray, pray to our Father and St. Francis Xavier that they will render me worthy. My Father, my Father, a single word of reply, one *fiat,* or at least one line alone which I receive from Your Reverence in which you give me some hope. It will be for me like a fire which will serve to light in me the worthy desire which God our Master deigned to communicate to me, as it were to give myself to Him, and to venture always more on the path of sanctity. With your paternal blessing I remain a faithful servant of Your Paternity.

[Signed] GREGORY MENGARINI

Rome
On the day of the holiest Christmas, 1839

Appendix B

Mengarini's Official Report for 1847
Containing an Account of the
Little Faro Rebellion

The village rebellion led by the Flathead brave, Little Faro, was an echo of the Indian protest against whites in the Oregon Territory which flared intermittently throughout the region during 1847. In his official annual report to the Father General of the Society of Jesus, Mengarini details the events, the inability of the chiefs to quell them and the eventual reunion of the factions.[1]

St. Mary's Mission
February 21, 1848

Father Gregory Mengarini to Father General
Paternity

Along with this letter is included for Your Paternity, the letter which I started to dispatch in September of last year, but which Father Joset was unable to mail for he received it in November after the mails had left. This overdue letter carries with it the pain you would have felt had you been able to witness the trials of St. Mary's Mission. It was but temporary as you will see from my second letter in which I shall explain the events and describe how I with the aid of Our Father *Facit nobilissi miserricordia suam,* which was, however, preceded by great tribulation.

The Flatheads who returned from the buffalo hunt somewhat after my return from the Coeur d'Alene, appeared somewhat more well-disposed. At the same time, the whites, not content with having usurped

---

[1] Mt. Sax., Vol. i, Fol. 5, p. 6, GASJ.

the lands of the savages, reintroduced the game of the hands, teaching
it to the younger Flatheads who they cunningly succeeded in luring to
the other side of the river. Two brothers then declared they were no
longer Frenchmen but Americans and in lowered voices began to crit-
icize their religion and the [illegible].

The youths then began to play in the village itself, near our house.
Several of the chiefs murmured against the resumption of this vice,
but they made little impression, and thus were satisfied simply to say,
"*Tsalgatt,* it is not good."

All these things were reported to me, and foreseeing that things
would get worse if the chiefs continued to behave as they did, I began
instructing them in particular and exhorting them strongly to do their
duty so that calm would reign over the community and it would not
be seduced. But one approach or another accomplished nothing.
Finally, when all the leaders as well as the subjects developed an
antagonism toward the whites, and toward one of the Flatheads who
had become good friends with them, then they wished the Father to
cast them out. Now, this friend of the whites who until now [illegible]
old things [illegible]. I will only say that this herald who announced
the end of penance and declared himself leader, caused great injury to
the missionary effort and for sometime greatly upset the relationship
between missionary and savage.

He, I now believe, took offense at a correction that the missionary
thought he had given with the best intention. On Sunday when all the
savages gathered in church to recite the rosary, he interfered and
began to harangue them publicly in the church, uttering the most in-
sulting things against the missionaries, yet in such a manner that I
understood nearly nothing. From that he went on to inveigh against
and complain against the chiefs. And not one (with the exception of
our interpreter Francis) shouted out any disapproval of this diatribe.
No one attempted to still this tirade except this one poor blind man,
nor did they demonstrate the slightest sign of disapproval.

When from several villagers I learned the extent of the scandal
given and the negative attitude of the chiefs, I decided that it was
necessary to give a little lesson to all, so as much to reveal to the
scandalizer the great harm done, as to give to the others a lesson
regarding the profanation of the house of God, I decided during the

night that the church would remain closed and we would not give benediction, thinking that thus I would finally shock them.

During that same day an epidemic of Smallpox erupted. A young girl died that evening. Again I called the chiefs and openly spoke to them, reminding them that forty others were dying. In other words, the toll appeared to be three times that of other years. Perhaps, I suggested, this was a warning from God to shock them into at least controlling the scandalous talk in church, even if they wished to do nothing more. If they did this, tomorrow we would say Mass. If they did nothing, we would not say Mass, but instead dismiss the people. There was one who went to the scandalizer and pleaded with him not to again enter the church [to interrupt], but the next day no attention was given. The scandalizer not only entered the church with braggadocio, but placed himself as close as possible to the altar amidst the chiefs, and assumed the air of being on the pulpit. Father Ravalli who was of the same opinion as I took the responsibility of saying Mass in order to prove to the savages that I was not alone in opposing them. Father Ravalli had already vested, the prayers had begun when we saw the scandalizer nearby. Ravalli interrupted the prayers, unvested, and dismissed the people. Then we announced that there would be no more prayer in church until one of the chiefs or someone else would come to the missionary with the assurance that the scandalizer would not again enter or appear.

The scandalizer was greatly praised by the two whites who claimed to be Americans and encouraged by them, he continued his harangue throughout the day, running about the village like a man possessed. He shouted at the missionaries and urged them to leave. Then he turned upon the chiefs calling them puppets (and not without cause).

But who would have thought that instead of a day or two to ventilate their grievances, instead three weeks would pass before there would be relief from this harassment. Frequently, men came running to complain that there was no one to impede this rabble rouser. But all ended with that for the chiefs appeared to be sleeping.

But in the meantime the scandalizer was struck with the disease. The throat, mouth and tongue swelled, yet he continued his attacks each day. And he recovered. But on that same day the youngest of his children who out of affection he had given his own name of *Sioux*

Taren, was attacked by a cancer [?] in the mouth which in three days spread across his face. It was accompanied by such a stench that all were obliged to leave the house. The fourth day he died. But instead of opening his father's eyes, this only served to harden him, and his invective became worse than ever, finally shouting that the prayers offered in the tent were as dry as buffalo sinew. Then the chiefs withdrew to deliberate. Four of these went to the house of the poor scandalizer imploring him to present himself before the great chief. But they were received with the greeting of puppets, and following this atheist's refusal, they retired one by one. One of the first went to report to the missionary that some wished to take action while the others did not.

Things were reduced to this extreme state. The missionaries were exhausted of resources. They had offered Masses and Holy Communions, had sought the prayers of the congregation offered to the Immaculate Heart of Mary, and had worked for months using all human means to shake the Flatheads, especially since many were dying each day from Smallpox.

Finally, God moved the heart of one man of advanced age, who suffered to see the extreme weakness of the chiefs. The day following their announced disagreement, he remained in the tent with the chiefs after prayer and in a fine forceful manner requested permission to address the scandalizer himself. Without much ceremony he prepared to act. The scandalizer, now seeing his opportunity at an end, allowed himself to be conducted like a lamb before the chiefs who flogged him and subjected him to a scathing exhortation. In a matter of one day all took on a new aspect.

Bibliography
and Index

Bibliography

MANUSCRIPTS

Franciscan Provincial Archives, Old Mission, Santa Barbara, California:
Letter from Rev. Gregory Mengarini, s.j., Feb. 7, 1861
Archives of the Society of Jesus, General Archives, Rome, Italy:
Rev. Michael Accolti, s.j., Letters
Rev. Gregory Mengarini, s.j., Letters and "Memorie delle Missioni delle Teste Piatte, 1848." (Unpublished Mss.)
(Microcopies of the above are in the Oregon Provincial Archives of the Society of Jesus, Gonzaga University)

Archives of the Oregon Province of the Society of Jesus, Gonzaga University, Spokane, Washington:
Anonymous, "St. Mary's Mission, Stevensville," (unpublished ms.)
O'Sullivan, Rev. John, s.j., "History of the Rocky Mountain Missions," (unpublished ms.)
Schoenberg, Rev. Wilfred P., s.j., "Memorandum Regarding St. Mary's Existing Log Church," (unpublished ms.)
Scrapbooks of newspaper clippings commemorating the centennial of the establishment of St. Mary's, as well as maps and photographs
Letters and papers of: Rev. Michael Accolti, s.j.; Rev. Adrian Hoecken, s.j.; Rev. Joseph Joset, s.j.; Rev. John Killeen, s.j.; Dr. John McLoughlin to Rev. Pierre Jean De Smet, s.j., Jan. 25, 1845; Rev. Gregory Mengarini, s.j.; Rev. John Nobili, s.j.; Rev. Nicolas Point, s.j.

UNPUBLISHED MASTERS' THESES

Forbis, Richard G. "Religious Acculturation of the Flathead Indians of Montana," Mont. St. Univ., 1950

Malan, Vernon D. "Language and Social Change Among the Flathead Indians," Mont. St. Univ., 1948

PERSONAL CORRESPONDENCE

Personal letters to Gloria R. Lothrop from: Mary Ann Bonino, Los Angeles, Sept. 16, 1969; Robert Dightman, Helena, Mont., June 6, 1968; Prof. Richard Daugherty, Pullman, Wash., Nov. 29, 1969; Michael Kogen, M.D., Los Angeles, June 6, 1968

Personal letters of Doyce B. Nunis, Jr. and William L. Davis, s.J. (courtesy of Professor Nunis)

PRINTED SOURCES

Anonymous. *La Medicina omiopatica considerata nel suo verro aspetto e in modo adatto alla commune intelligenza.* Milan, Italy: N.p., 1838

——. "Obituary, Gregory Mengarini, s.J.," *The Woodstock Letters: A Record of Current Events and Historical Notes Connected with the College and Missions of the Society of Jesus,* XVI (1886), pp. 93-97

——. *Santa Clara College, 1851-1912.* San Jose: University Press, 1912

——. "Weekly Talk," *The Woodstock Letters,* XX (1886), p. 356

——. "Jesuit Missions in California," *The Woodstock Letters,* XX (Feb. 1891), pp. 347-68

Alvord, Bernard. *Report Concerning the Indians in the Territories of Oregon and Washington.* H.R. Ex. Doc. No. 75 (Serial No. 36), 34th Cong., 3rd Sess. Wash., D.C., 1857, pp. 10-22

"Apostle of the Iroquois who Brought Faith to Indian," *Montana Catholic Register, Western Edition* (Aug. 1941)

Bagley, Clarence B. *Early Catholic Missions in Old Oregon.* Seattle: Lowman and Hanford Co., 1932

Bain, Read. "Educational Plans and Efforts by Methodists in Oregon to 1860," *Oreg. Hist. Quar.,* XXI (Mar. 1920), pp. 63-94

Barclay, Wade C. *History of the Methodist Missions.* 3 vols. New York: Board of Missions, 1950

Barry, Louise. "Kansas Before 1854: A Revised Annals," *Kan. Hist. Quar.,* XXIX (Spring 1963), pp. 45-46

Berkhoffer, Robert F. *Salvation and the Savage, An Analysis of Protestant Missions and American Indian Response, 1787-1862.* Lexington, Ky: Univ. of Ky. Press, 1965

Bidwell, John. "The First Immigrant Train to California," *The Century Illustrated Monthly Magazine,* XLI (Nov. 1890), pp. 106-30

Bischoff, William N. *Jesuits in Old Oregon, A Sketch of Jesuit Activities in the Pacific Northwest, 1840-1940.* Caldwell, Id: The Caxton Printers, 1945

Blossom, Robert. "First Presbyterianism on the Pacific Coast," *Oreg. Hist. Quar.,* XV (June 1914), pp. 81-103

Blue, George V. "Green's Missionary Report on Oregon," *Oreg. Hist. Quar.,* XXX (Sept. 1929), pp. 227-45

Brown, William C. *The Indian Side of the Story.* Spokane, Wash: C. W. Hill Pntg. Co., 1961

Buchanan, Charles M. "The Catholic Ladder," *The Indian Sentinel,* VII (Winter 1918), p. 167

Burns, Robert Ignatius. *The Jesuits and the Indian Wars of the Northwest.* New Haven and London: Yale Univ. Pr., 1966

Butler, B. Robert. "Prehistory of the Dice Game in the Southern Plateau," *Tebiwa,* II (Mar. 1958), pp. 63-67

Campbell, Thomas J. "Father De Smet," *The Indian Sentinel,* VI (Winter 1916), pp. 4-6

———. *The Jesuits, 1534-1921.* 2 vols. New York: The Encyclopedia Press, 1921

Casagrande, A. Salvatore. *De Claribus Sodalibus Provincia Taurinensis, Societatis Ieus, Commentarii.* Turin, Italy: Guilio Spierani e Figli, 1906

Chittenden, Hiram M. *The American Fur Trade of the Far West.* 2 vols. New York: Press of the Pioneers, Inc., 1935

———, and Richardson, Alfred D. (eds.). *Life, Letters and Travels of Father Pierre-Jean De Smet, S.J., 1801-1872.* 4 vols. New York: Francis P. Harper, 1905

Clark, Ella E. *Indian Legends from the Northern Rockies.* Norman, Okla: Univ. of Okla. Pr., 1966

Corley, Patricia. *The Story of Saint Mary's Mission.* Oakland, Calif: Tribune Press, 1941

Coues, Elliot (ed.). *Manuscript Journals of Alexander Henry and David Thompson.* 3 vols. New York: Francis P. Harper, 1897

Cox, Ross. *Adventures on the Columbia River.* 2 vols. New York, 1832. Republished as *The Columbia River,* ed. by Edgar I. and Jane R. Stewart. Norman, Okla: Univ. of Okla. Pr., 1957

Cullen, Stewart. "Games of the North American Indians," *Bureau of American Ethnology, Twenty-fourth Annual Report.* Wash., D.C: Govt. Pntg. Office, 1902-1903, pp. 447-79

Cullen, William J. to Nathaniel G. Taylor, *Report of the Commissioner of Indian Affairs.* Wash., D.C: Dept. of the Int., 1868

Curtis, Edward S. *Indian Days of Long Ago.* Yonkers, N.Y: World Publishing Co., 1915

——. *The North American Indians, Being a Series of Volumes Picturing and Describing the Indians of the United States and Alaska.* Ed. by Frederick W. Hodge. 20 vols. Seattle, Wash. and Cambridge, Mass: Priv. printed, 1907-1913

Davis, William L., S.J. *A History of St. Ignatius Mission, An Outpost of Catholic Culture on the Montana Frontier.* Spokane: C. W. Hill Pntg. Co., 1952

——. "Peter John De Smet, Missionary to the Potawatomi," *Pacific Northwest Quar.,* XXXIII (Apr. 1942), pp. 123-52

——. "Peter John De Smet, the Years of Preparation, 1801-1837," *Pacific Northwest Quar.,* XXXII (Apr. 1941), pp. 167-96

Davison, Stanley M. "Worker in God's Wilderness," *Montana Magazine of Western History,* VII (Jan. 1957), pp. 8-17

De Smet, Peter John. *Letters and Sketches with a Narrative of a Year's Residence Among the Indian Tribes of the Rocky Mountains.* Phila: King and Baire, 1843

——. *Oregon Missions and Travels in the Rocky Mountains in 1845-46.* Paris: Poussielgue-Rusand, 1847

——. *Voyages aux Montagnes Rocheuses.* New ed. Brussels: Victor Devaux, 1873

——. *Western Missions and Missionaries, A Series of Letters of Rev. Jean-Pierre De Smet.* New York: J. B. Kirker, Dunnigan and Bros., 1863

DeVoto, Bernard. *Across the Wide Missouri.* Boston: Houghton Mifflin Co., 1947

——. *Course of Empire.* Boston: Houghton Mifflin Co., 1952

Donnelly, William. "Nineteenth Century Jesuit Reductions in the United States," *Mid-America,* XVII (Jan. 1935), pp. 72-81

Driver, Harold C. *Indians of North America.* Chicago: Univ. of Chicago Pr., 1961

Drury, Clifford M. (ed.). *The Diaries and Letters of Henry H. Spalding and Asa Bowen Smith Relating to the Nez Perce Mission.* Glendale, Calif: Arthur H. Clark Co., 1958

——. *Elkanah and Mary Walker.* Caldwell, Id: Caxton Printers, 1940

——. *First White Women Over the Rockies.* 3 vols. Glendale, Calif: Arthur H. Clark Co., 1963-1966

——. *Henry Harmon Spalding.* Caldwell, Id: Caxton Printers, 1940

——. *Marcus and Narcissa Whitman.* 2 vols. Glendale, Calif: Arthur H. Clark Co., 1973

——. "The Nez Perce Delegation of 1831," *Oreg. Hist. Quar.,* XL (Sept. 1939), pp. 283-87

——. "Oregon Indians of the Red River School," *Pacific Hist. Review,* XXIX (Mar. 1938), pp. 50-60

——. "Protestant Missionaries in Oregon: A Bibliographic Survey," *Oreg. Hist. Quar.,* L (Sept. 1949), pp. 209-17

——. "Some Aspects of Presbyterian History in Oregon," *Oreg. Hist. Quar.,* LV (June 1954), pp. 145-59

Eells, M. "Tradition of the 'Deluge' Among the Tribes of the Northwest," *American Antiquarian,* I (Apr. 1878), pp. 70-72

Elliott, Thompson C. "Religion Among the Flatheads," *Oreg. Hist. Quar.,* XXXVII (Mar. 1938), pp. 1-8

Ewers, John C. *The Blackfeet, Raiders on the Northwestern Plains.* Norman, Okla: Univ. of Okla. Pr., 1950

——. *Gustavus Sohon's Portraits of Flathead and Pend d'Oreille Indians, 1854.* Wash., D.C: Smithsonian Misc. Coll., Vol. 110, No. 7, 1948

Fahey, John. *The Flathead Indians.* Norman, Okla: Univ. of Okla. Pr., 1973

Finnegan, George. "Quest of Indians for Blackrobe," *The Tablet,* (n.d.), Jesuit Arch., Gonzaga Univ.

Fitzpatrick, Thomas. "Letter to Thomas H. Harvey," Upper Platte Agency File, 1846-1851, Microcopy, Nat. Arch., Wash., D.C.

Forbis, Richard. "The Flathead Apostasy," *Montana Mag. of Western Hist.,* IV (Winter 1951), pp. 35-40

Francesca, Sister Mary. "Semi-Centennial of Father De Smet," *The Indian Sentinel,* III (Spring 1923), pp. 35-40

Garraghan, Gilbert J. *The Jesuits of the Middle United States.* 3 vols. New York: J. J. Little and Ives Co., 1938

——. "Nicolas Point, Jesuit Missionary to Montana in the Forties," in *The Trans-Mississippi West.* Ed. by James R. Willard and Colin B. Goodykoontz. Boulder, Colo: Univ. of Colo. Hist. Coll., 1930, pp. 43-63

Gass, Patrick. *A Journal of the Voyages and Travels of a Corps of Discovery.* Pittsburg: Printed by Zadok Cramer, for David M'Keehan, Publ. and Proprietor, 1807

Ghent, William J. *The Early Far West.* New York: Longman's, Green and Co., 1931

Gibbs, George. *Reports of Explorations and Surveys to Ascertain the Most Practicable and Economical Route for a Railroad from the Mississippi River to the Pacific Ocean.* 12 vols. Wash., D.C: Govt. Pntg. Office, 1855-60

——. "Tribes of Western Washington and Northwestern Oregon," John Wesley Powell, ed., *Contributions to North American Ethnology.* Wash., D.C: Dept. of the Int., 1877. Pp. 227-368

Giorda, Joseph; Bandini, Joseph; and Mengarini, Gregory. *A Dictionary of the Kalispel or Flathead Language.* St. Ignatius, Mont: St. Ignatius Print, 1877-1879

Graham, R. B. Cunningham. *Vanished Arcadia.* London: Wm. Heinemann, 1901

Gray, Wm. Henry. *A History of Oregon, 1792-1849, Drawn from Personal Observations and Authentic Information.* 2 vols. Portland, Oreg: Harris and Holman, 1870

Griswold, Gillett, and Larom, David. *The Hell Gate Survey.* Missoula, Mont: Mont. St. Univ., 1954

Gunther, Erna. "Westward Movement of Some Plains Traits," *American Anthropologist,* LII (Apr.-June 1950), pp. 174-80

Hafen, LeRoy R. (ed.). *The Mountain Men and the Fur Trade of the Far West; Biographical Sketches of the Participants by Scholars of the Subject and with an Introduction by the Editor.* 10 vols. Glendale, Calif: The Arthur H. Clark Co., 1964-72

Hafen, LeRoy R., and Ghent, Wm. *Broken Hand, The Life Story of Thomas Fitzpatrick, Chief of the Mountain Men.* Denver: The Old West Publ. Co., 1931

Hagen, William T. *American Indians.* Chicago: The Univ. of Chic. Pr., 1961

Harney, Michael P. *The Jesuits in History.* New York: The American Press, 1941

Himes, George H. "Beginnings of Christianity in Oregon," *Oreg. Hist. Quar.,* XX (June 1919), pp. 159-72

Hodge, Frederick W. (ed.). *Handbook of American Indians North of Mexico.* 2 vols. *Bulletin 30 of the Bu. of Amer. Ethn.,* Parts 1 and 2. Wash., D.C: Govt. Pntg. Off., 1942

Hoffman, William J. "Vocabulary of the Salish Language," *Proceedings of the Amer. Phil. Soc.,* XXIII (Apr. 1886), pp. 361-71

Holmes, Kenneth L. "Mount St. Helens' Recent Eruptions," *Oreg. Hist. Quar.,* LVI (Sept. 1955), pp. 197-210

Hughes, Thomas. *History of the Society of Jesus in North America, Colonial and Federal Documents.* 2 vols. New York: Gregg Intl., 1910

Irvine, Caleb E. "Famous Indian Footrace," *Contributions to the Hist. Soc. of Mont.,* VI (1917), pp. 479-80

Jessett, Thomas E. *Chief Spokane Garry.* Minneapolis: T. S. Denison, 1960

Johnson, Olga W. *Flathead and Kootenay.* Glendale, Calif: Arthur H. Clark Co., 1969

Joset, Joseph, S.J. "Washington Territory, Then and Now," *The Woodstock Letters,* XII (May 1883), pp. 167-79

Jung, Andrew M. *Jesuit Missions Among the American Tribes of Rocky Mountain Indians.* Spokane, Wash: Gonzaga Univ. Pr., 1925

Kenneally, Finbar. *United States Documents in the Propaganda Fide Archives, A Calendar.* 6 vols. Wash., D.C: Wash. Acad. of Amer. Franciscan Hist., 1975

Kip, William J. *The Early Jesuit Missions in North America, Compiled and Translated from the Letters of the French Jesuits with Notations.* Albany, N.Y: Wiley and Putnam, 1846

Kroeber, A[lfred] L. *Anthropology*. New York: 1923. Rev. ed. New York: Harcourt Brace, 1948

"Letter from John Maguire," *Daily Territorial Enterprise* (Virginia City, Nev.), June 22, 1875, cited in *Contributions to the Hist. Soc. of Mont.*, VIII (1917), pp. 152-53

Lewis, Oscar. "The Effects of White Contact Upon the Blackfoot Culture with Special Reference to the Role of the Fur Trade," *Monographs of the Amer. Ethn. Soc.*, VI (1942), pp. 1-73

Mallet, Maj. Edward. "The Origin of the Flathead Mission of the Rocky Mountains," *Records of the Amer. Cath. Hist. Soc.*, II (1889), pp. 174-205

McDonald, Angus. "A Few Items of the West," *The Wash. Hist. Quar.*, VII (July 1917), pp. 187-201

McHugh, Michael. "A Dream Went West," in *I Lift My Lamp*, ed. by John B. Leary. Westminster, N.Y: Newman Press, 1955. Pp. 158-75

Mengarini, Gregory. "Indians of Oregon," *Journal of the Anth. Inst. of N.Y.*, I (1871-72), pp. 81-88

——. "The Rocky Mountain Memoir of Fr. Mengarini," *The Woodstock Letters*, XVII (1888), pp. 298-309; XVIII (1889), pp. 25-43, 142-52

——. *A Selish or Flathead Grammar*. New York: Cramoisy Press, 1861

——. "Vocabulary of the Santa Clara," in John Wesley Powell (ed.), *Contributions to North American Ethnology*. Wash., D.C: Dept. of the Int., 1877. Pp. 538-49

——. "Vocabulary of the Shwoyelpi, S'chitzui, and Salish Proper," in John Wesley Powell (ed.), *Contributions to North American Ethnology*. Wash., D.C: Dept. of the Int., 1877. Pp. 267-82

Merriam, Alan P. *Ethnomusicology of the Flathead Indians*. Chicago: Aldine Publ. Co., 1967

Missione Della Provincia Torinese Della Compagnia Di Gesu Nelle Montagne Rocciose Della America Settentrionale. Turin, Italy: Guilio Spierani e Figli, 1863 and 1887.

Morgan, Lewis H. "Indian Migrations," in *The Indian Miscellany*, ed. by Wm. W. Beach. Albany, N.Y: N.p., 1877. Pp. 158-257

Nunis, Doyce B., Jr. (ed.). *Josiah Belden, 1841 California Overland Pioneer: His Memoir and Early Letters.* Georgetown, Calif: Talisman Press, 1962

O'Connor, Bishop James. "The Flathead Indians," *Records of the Amer. Cath. Hist. Soc.,* III (1888-91), pp. 85-110

O'Connor, Thomas. "Pierre De Smet, Frontier Missionary," *Mid-America,* XVII (July 1935), pp. 191-97

O'Hara, Edwin V. "De Smet in the Oregon Territory," *Oreg. Hist. Quar.,* X (Sept. 1909), pp. 42-54

Oliphant, J. Orin. "George Simpson and the Oregon Missions," *Pacific Hist. Rev.,* XXVIII (Sept. 1937), pp. 213-48

Palladino, Lawrence B. "Historical Notes on the Flathead," *The Indian Sentinel,* I (Oct. 1919), pp. 6-16

——. *Indian and White in the Northwest, A History of Catholicity in Montana, 1831 to 1891.* 2nd ed. Lancaster, Pa: Wickersham Publ. Co., 1922

Parker, Samuel. *Journal of an Exploring Tour Beyond the Rocky Mountains.* 3rd ed. Ithaca, N.Y: Mack, Andrus, and Woodruff, 1842

Partoll, Albert J. "The Flathead-Salish Name in Montana Nomenclature," *Montana Mag. of Western Hist.,* I (Jan. 1951), pp. 37-48

——. (ed.). "Mengarini's Narrative to the Rockies," *Frontier and Midland,* XVIII (1938), pp. 193-202, 258-66. Reprinted in *Sources of Northwest History,* No. 25, Missoula, Mont: Mont. St. Univ. Pr., n.d.; and *Frontier Omnibus,* ed. by John W. Hakola, Missoula, Mont: Mont. St. Univ. Pr., 1962

Point, Nicolas. "Recollections of the Rocky Mountain Missions," *The Woodstock Letters,* XI (Sept. 1882), pp. 298-321

——. *Wilderness Kingdom, Life in the Rockies 1840-1847. The Journals and Paintings of Nicolas Point.* Ed. and trans. by Joseph P. Donnelly. New York: Holt, Rinehart and Winston, 1967

Post, Herbert A. "Among the Flathead," *The Indian Sentinel,* II (Jan. 1920), pp. 48-51

Prando, Peter. "Letter from Father Peter Prando," *The Woodstock Letters,* XII (Jan. 1883), pp. 25-37

Rappagliosi, P. Filippo. *Memorie del Padre Filippo Rappagliosi.* Rome: Tipografia di Bernardo Marini, 1879

Reilly, Louis W. "Father Ravalli, Pioneer Indian Missionary," *Catholic World,* CXXV (Apr. 1927), pp. 67-73

Ronan, Maj. Peter. *Historical Sketch of the Flathead Indian Nation from the Year 1813 to 1890.* Helena, Mont: Jour. Publ. Co., 1890

Saum, Lewis O. *The Fur Trader and the Indian.* Seattle and London: Univ. of Wash. Pr., 1965

Schaeffer, Claude. "The First Jesuit Mission to the Flatheads, 1840-1850, a Study in Culture Conflicts," *Pacific Northwest Quar.,* XXVIII (July 1937), pp. 227-50

Schoenberg, Wilfred A. *Jesuit Mission Presses in the Pacific Northwest, a History and Bibliography of Imprints, 1876-1899.* Portland: Champoeg Press, 1957

——. *The Jesuits in Montana.* Portland: The Oregon-Jesuit, 1960

Shea, John Gilmary. *History of the Catholic Missions Among the Indian Tribes of the United States, 1529-1854.* New York: T. W. Strong, 1854

Sommervogel, Carlos (ed.). *Bibliotheque de la Compagnie de Jesus.* 11 vols. Brussels and Paris: Librarie de la Societe, 1890-1919

Suttles, Walter, and Elmendorf, Wm. W. "Linguistic Evidence for Salish Pre-history," in *Symposium on Language and Culture,* Proc. of Ann. Spring Mtg. Wash., D.C., 1963, pp. 41-52

Swadeesh, James A. "Salish Internal Relationships," *Intl. Jour. of Amer. Linguistics,* XVI (Sept. 1951), pp. 106-27

Swanton, John R. (comp.) *The Indian Tribes of North America,* Bur. of Amer. Ethn., *Bulletin no. 145,* Wash., D.C: Govt. Pntg. Off., 1952

Teit, James A. *The Salishan Tribes of the Western Plateaus,* Bur. of Amer. Ethn., *Forty-fifth Ann. Rept.* Ed. by Franz Boas. Wash., D.C: Govt. Pntg. Off., 1927-28

Thompson, David. *David Thompson's Narrative of Explorations in Western America, 1784-1812,* ed. by J. B. Tyrrell. Toronto: Champlain Society, 1916

Thwaites, Reuben Gold. "Discovery of the Source of the Columbia River," ed. by T[hompson] C. Elliott, *Oreg. Hist. Quar.,* XXVI (Mar. 1925), pp. 23-49

—— (ed.). *Early Western Travels*. 32 vols. Cleveland: Arthur H. Clark Co., 1904-1907

—— (ed.). *The Jesuit Relations and Allied Documents, Travels and Explorations of Jesuit Missioners in New France, 1610-1791*. 73 vols. Cleveland: Burrows Bros. Co., 1896-1901

Turney-High, Henry Holbert. "The Bluejay Dance," *Amer. Anth.,* xxxv (Apr. 1933), pp. 103-07

——. *The Flathead Indians of Montana*. Menasha, Wis: Memoir 48 of the Amer. Anth. Assoc., 1941

United States Dept. of the Int. *Biographical and Historical Index of American Indian and Persons Involved in Indian Affairs*. 8 vols. Boston: C. K. Hall, 1966

Vita Functi in Societati Iesu, 7 Augusti 1814-7 Augusti 1914. Paris: N.p., 1897

Vita Functi in Societati Iesu, Provincia Oregiensis. Portland: Sentinel Printery, 1960

Voeglin, Carl F. "North American Indian Languages Still Spoken and Their Relationships," in *Language, Culture and Personality,* ed. by Leslie Spier and Alan S. Hallowell. Menasha, Wis: Sapir Memorial Publication Fund, 1950

Weisel, George F. "Animal Names, Anatomical Terms, and Some Ethnozoology of the Flathead Indians," *Jour. of the Wash. Acad. of Sciences,* xlii (1952), pp. 345-55.

——. "The Ram's Horn Tree and Other Medicine Trees of the Flathead Indians," *Montana Mag. of Western Hist.,* i (Summer 1951), pp. 5-14

——. "Ten Animal Myths of the Flathead Indians," *Anthropology and Sociology Papers,* No. 18, Mont. St. Univ. Mimeographed copy, n.d., n.p.

Wilkes, George. *A History of Oregon, Geographical and Political, etc. To Which is Added a Journal of the Events of the Celebrated Emigrating Expedition of 1843*. New York: W. H. Colyer, 1845

Williams, Joseph. *Narrative of a Tour from the State of Indiana to the Oregon Territory in the Years 1841-42,* with an introduction by James C. Bell. Cincinnati: Priv. pntd., 1845

Wissler, Clark. *American Indian*. 3rd ed. New York: Oxford Univ. Pr. N.Y., Inc., 1938

Work, John. "Diary, June 21-Nov. 1, 1825, Journal of John Work,"
ed. by Thompson C. Elliott, *Pac. Northwest Quar.,* v (Oct. 1914),
pp. 83-115; (July 1914), pp. 163-91; (Oct. 1914), pp. 258-87; vi
(Jan. 1915), pp. 26-49

NEWSPAPERS

Christian Advocate (N.Y.), Mar. 1, 1833
Eastern Montana Reporter (location unknown), Dec. 24, 1950
Great Falls (Mont.) *Tribune,* Sept. 30, 1950; July 28, 1968
Montana Catholic Register – Western Edition (Helena, Mont.),
Aug., 1941
Montana Standard (Helena, Mont.), June 21, 1941
Pioneer and Democrat (Olympia, Wash.), Jan. 27, 1855
San Francisco (Calif.) *Morning Call,* Sept. 25, 1886
Stevensville (Mont.) *Register,* Dec. 23, 1909
Sunday Missoulian (Missoula, Mont.), Aug. 24, 1941

Index